The
Mother
of All
Questions

The Mother of All Questions

Rebecca Solnit

Images by Paz de la Calzada

Haymarket Books
Chicago, Illinois

Haymarket Books
PO Box 180165
Chicago, IL 60618
773-583-7884
info@haymarketbooks.org
www.haymarketbooks.org

ISBN: 978-1-60846-740-2

Trade distribution:
In the US, through Consortium Book Sales and Distribution,
www.cbsd.com
In Canada, Publishers Group Canada, www.pgcbooks.ca

Special discounts are available for bulk purchases by organizations
and institutions.

Please contact Haymarket Books for more information at 773-583-7884
or info@haymarketbooks.org.

This book was published with the generous support of Lannan
Foundation and the Wallace Action Fund.

Cover design by Abby Weintraub.

Library of Congress Cataloging-in-Publication Data is available.

Printed in Canada by union labor.

10 9 8 7 6 5 4 3 2

Contents

In hope we keep going
with love for the newcomers
and their beautiful noise:
Atlas
Ella and Maya
Isaac and Martin
Berkeley
Brooke, Dylan, and Solomon,
Daisy and Jake;
and thanks to the readers
and to the hellraisers

Introduction

The longest and newest essay in this book is about silence, and I began it thinking I was writing about the many ways women are silenced. I soon realized that the ways men are silenced were an inseparable part of my subject, and that each of us exists in a complex of many kinds of silence, including the reciprocal silences we call gender roles. This is a feminist book, yet it is not a book about women's experience alone but about all of ours—men, women, children, and people who are challenging the binaries and boundaries of gender.

This book deals with men who are ardent feminists as well as men who are serial rapists, and it is written in the recognition that all categories are leaky and we must use them provisionally. It addresses the rapid social changes of a revitalized feminist movement in North America and around the world that is not merely altering the laws. It's changing our understanding of consent, power, rights, gender, voice, and representation. It is a gorgeously transformative movement led in particular by the young, on campuses, on social media, in the streets, and my admiration for this fearlessly unapologetic new generation of feminists and human rights activists is vast. As is my fear of the backlash against it, a backlash that is itself evidence of the threat feminism, as part of the broader project of liberation, poses to patriarchy and the status quo.

This book is a tour through carnage, a celebration of liberation and solidarity, insight and empathy, and an investigation of the terms and tools with which we might explore all these things.

The Mother
of All Questions

(2015)

I gave a talk on Virginia Woolf a few years ago. During the question period that followed, the subject that seemed to most interest a number of people was whether Woolf should have had children. I answered the question dutifully, noting that Woolf apparently considered having children early in her marriage, after seeing the delight that her sister, Vanessa Bell, took in her own. But over time Woolf came to see reproduction as unwise, perhaps because of her own psychological instability. Or maybe, I suggested, she wanted to be a writer and to give her life over to her art, which she did with extraordinary success. In the talk I had quoted with approval her description of murdering "the Angel in the House," the inner voice that tells many women to be self-sacrificing handmaidens to domesticity and the male ego. I was surprised that advocating for throttling the spirit of conventional femininity should lead to this conversation.

What I should have said to that crowd was that our interrogation of Woolf's reproductive status was a soporific and pointless detour from the magnificent questions her work poses. (I think at

3

some point I said, "Fuck this shit," which carried the same general message, and moved everyone on from the discussion.) After all, many people make babies; only one made *To the Lighthouse* and *Three Guineas*, and we were discussing Woolf because of the latter.

The line of questioning was familiar enough to me. A decade ago, during a conversation that was supposed to be about a book I had written on politics, the British man interviewing me insisted that instead of talking about the products of my mind, we should talk about the fruit of my loins, or the lack thereof. Onstage, he hounded me about why I didn't have children. No answer I gave could satisfy him. His position seemed to be that I must have children, that it was incomprehensible that I did not, and so we had to talk about why I didn't, rather than about the books I did have.

When I got off stage, my Scottish publisher's publicist—slight, twenty-something, wearing pink ballet slippers and a pretty engagement ring, was scowling in fury. "He would never ask a man that," she spat. She was right. (I use that now, framed as a question, to stymie some of the questioners: "Would you ask a man that?") Such questions seem to come out of the sense that there are not *women*, the 51 percent of the human species who are as diverse in their wants and as mysterious in their desires as the other 49 percent, only *Woman*, who must marry, must breed, must let men in and babies out, like some elevator for the species. At their heart these questions are not questions but assertions that we who fancy ourselves individuals, charting our own courses, are wrong. Brains are individual phenomena producing wildly varying products; uteruses bring forth one kind of creation.

As it happens, there are many reasons why I don't have children: I am very good at birth control; though I love children and adore aunthood, I also love solitude; I was raised by unhappy, unkind people, and I wanted neither to replicate their form of parenting nor to create human beings who might feel about me the way that

I sometimes felt about my begetters; the planet is unable to sustain more first-world people, and the future is very uncertain; and I really wanted to write books, which as I've done it is a fairly consuming vocation. I'm not dogmatic about not having kids. I might have had them under other circumstances and been fine—as I am now.

Some people want kids but don't have them for various private reasons, medical, emotional, financial, professional; others don't want kids, and that's not anyone's business either. Just because the question can be answered doesn't mean that anyone is obliged to answer it, or that it ought to be asked. The interviewer's question to me was indecent, because it presumed that women should have children, and that a woman's reproductive activities were naturally public business. More fundamentally, the question assumed that there was only one proper way for a woman to live.

But even to say that there's one proper way may be putting the case too optimistically, given that mothers are consistently found wanting, too. A mother may be treated like a criminal for leaving her child alone for five minutes, even if that child's father has left it alone for several years. Some mothers have told me that having children caused them to be treated as bovine nonintellects who should be disregarded. A lot of women I know have been told that they cannot be taken seriously professionally because they will go off and reproduce at some point. And many mothers who do succeed professionally are presumed to be neglecting someone. There is no good answer to how to be a woman; the art may instead lie in how we refuse the question.

We talk about open questions, but there are closed questions, too, questions to which there is only one right answer, at least as far as the interrogator is concerned. These are questions that push you into the herd or nip at you for diverging from it, questions that contain their own answers and whose aim is enforcement and punishment. One of my goals in life is to become truly rabbinical, to be able to answer closed questions with open questions, to have the internal authority to be a good gatekeeper when intruders approach, and to at least remember to ask, "Why are you asking that?" This, I've found, is always a good answer to an unfriendly question, and closed questions tend to be unfriendly. But on the day of my interrogation about having babies, I was taken by surprise (and severely jet-lagged), and so I was left to wonder: Why do such bad questions so predictably get asked?

Maybe part of the problem is that we have learned to ask the wrong things of ourselves. Our culture is steeped in a kind of pop psychology whose obsessive question is: Are you happy? We ask it so reflexively that it seems natural to wish that a pharmacist with a time machine could deliver a lifetime supply of antidepressants to Bloomsbury, so that an incomparable feminist prose stylist could be reoriented to produce litters of Woolf babies.

Questions about happiness generally assume that we know what a happy life looks like. Happiness is often described as the result of having a great many ducks lined up in a row—spouse, offspring, private property, erotic experiences—even though a millisecond of reflection will bring to mind countless people who have all those things and are still miserable.

We are constantly given one-size-fits-all formulas, but those formulas fail, often and hard. Nevertheless, we are given them again. And again and again. They become prisons and punishments; the prison of the imagination traps many in the prison of a life that is correctly aligned with the recipes and yet is entirely miserable.

The problem may be a literary one: we are given a single story line about what makes a good life, even though not a few who follow that story line have bad lives. We speak as though there is one good plot with one happy outcome, while the myriad forms a life can take flower—and wither—all around us.

Even those who live out the best version of the familiar story line might not find happiness as their reward. This is not necessarily a bad thing. I know a woman who was lovingly married for seventy years. She has had a long, meaningful life that she has lived according to her principles, and she is loved and respected by her descendants. But I wouldn't call her happy; her compassion for the vulnerable and concern for the future have given her a despondent worldview. What she has had instead of happiness requires better language to describe. There are entirely different criteria for a good life that might matter more to a person—loving and being loved or having satisfaction, honor, meaning, depth, engagement, hope.

Part of my own endeavor as a writer has been to find ways to value what is elusive and overlooked, to describe nuances and shades of meaning, to celebrate public life and solitary life, and—in John Berger's phrase—to find "another way of telling," which is part of why getting clobbered by the same old ways of telling is disheartening.

The conservative "defense of marriage," which is really nothing more than a defense of the old hierarchical arrangement that straight marriage was before feminists began to reform it, is sadly not just the property of conservatives. Too many in this society are entrenched in the devout belief that there is something magically awesome for children about the heterosexual two-parent household, which leads many people to stay in miserable marriages that are destructive for everyone within range. I know people who long hesitated to leave horrible marriages because the old recipe insists that somehow a situation that is terrible for one or both parents will be beneficent for the children. Even women with violently abusive spouses are often urged to stay in situations that are supposed to be so categorically wonderful that the details don't matter. Form wins out over content. And yet I've seen the joy of divorce and the myriad forms happy families can take, over and over and over, from one parent and one child to innumerable forms of multiple households and extended families.

After I wrote a book about myself and my mother, who married a brutal professional man and had four children and often seethed with rage and misery, I was ambushed by an interviewer who asked whether my abusive father was the reason I had failed to find a life partner. Her question was freighted with astonishing assumptions about what I had intended to do with my life and her right to intrude upon that life. The book, *The Faraway Nearby*, was, I thought, in a quiet, roundabout way about my long journey toward a really nice life, and an attempt to reckon with my mother's fury, including the origin of that fury in her entrapment in conventional feminine roles and expectations.

I have done what I set out to do in my life, and what I set out to do was not what my mother or the interviewer presumed. I set out to write books, to be surrounded by generous, brilliant people, and to have great adventures. Men—romances, flings, and long-term relationships—have been some of those adventures, and so have remote deserts, arctic seas, mountaintops, uprisings and disasters, and the exploration of ideas, archives, records, and lives.

Society's recipes for fulfillment seem to cause a great deal of unhappiness, both in those who are stigmatized for being unable or unwilling to carry them out and in those who obey but don't find happiness. Of course there are people with very standard-issue lives who are very happy. I know some of them, just as I know very happy childless and celibate monks, priests, and abbesses, gay divorcees, and everything in between. Last summer my friend Emma was walked down the aisle by her father, with his husband following right behind on Emma's mother's arm; the four of them, plus Emma's new husband, are an exceptionally loving and close-knit family engaged in the pursuit of justice through politics. This summer, both of the weddings I went to had two grooms and no brides; at the first, one of the grooms wept because he had been excluded from the right to marry for most of his life, and he had never thought he would see his own wedding.

Still, the same old questions come buzzing around—though they often seem less like questions than a sort of enforcement system. In the traditional worldview happiness is essentially private and selfish. Reasonable people pursue their self-interest, and when they do so successfully they are supposed to be happy. The very definition of what it means to be human is narrow, and altruism, idealism, and public life (except in the forms of fame, status, or material success) have little place on the shopping list. The idea that a life should seek meaning seldom emerges; not only are the standard activities assumed to be inherently meaningful, they are treated as the only meaningful options.

One of the reasons people lock onto motherhood as a key to feminine identity is the belief that children are the way to fulfill your capacity to love. But there are so many things to love besides one's own offspring, so many things that need love, so much other work love has to do in the world.

While many people question the motives of the childless, who are taken to be selfish for refusing the sacrifices that come with parenthood, they often neglect to note that those who love their children intensely may have less love left for the rest of the world. Christina Lupton, a writer who is also a mother, recently described some of the things she relinquished when motherhood's consuming tasks had her in their grasp, including

> all the ways of tending to the world that are less easily validated
> than parenting, but which are just as fundamentally necessary for
> children to flourish. I mean here the writing and inventing and
> the politics and the activism; the reading and the public speaking

and the protesting and the teaching and the filmmaking.... Most of the things I value most, and from which I trust any improvements in the human condition will come, are violently incompatible with the actual and imaginative work of childcare.

One of the fascinating things about Edward Snowden's sudden appearance a few years ago was the inability of many people to comprehend why a young man might give up on the recipe for happiness—high wages, secure job, Hawaiian home—to become the world's most sought-after fugitive. Their premise seemed to be that since all people are selfish, Snowden's motive must be a self-serving pursuit of attention or money.

During the first rush of commentary, Jeffrey Toobin, the *New Yorker's* legal expert, wrote that Snowden was "a grandiose narcissist who deserves to be in prison." Another pundit announced, "I think what we have in Edward Snowden is just a narcissistic young man who has decided he is smarter than the rest of us." Others assumed that he was revealing US government secrets because he had been paid by an enemy country.

Snowden seemed like a man from another century. In his initial communications with journalist Glenn Greenwald he called himself Cincinnatus—after the Roman statesman who acted for the good of his society without seeking self-advancement. This was a clue that Snowden formed his ideals and models far from the standard-issue formulas for happiness. Other eras and cultures often asked different questions from the ones we ask now: What is the most meaningful thing you can do with your life? What's your contribution to the world or your community? Do you live according to your principles? What will your legacy be? What does your life mean? Maybe our obsession with happiness is a way not to ask those other questions, a way to ignore how spacious our lives can be, how effective our work can be, and how far-reaching our love can be.

There is a paradox at the heart of the happiness question. Todd Kashdan, a psychology professor at George Mason University, reported a few years ago on studies that concluded that people who think being happy is important are more likely to become depressed: "Organizing your life around trying to become happier, making happiness the primary objective of life, gets in the way of actually becoming happy."

I did finally have my rabbinical moment in Britain. After the jet lag was over, I was interviewed onstage by a woman with a plummy, fluting accent. "So," she trilled, "you've been wounded by humanity and fled to the landscape for refuge." The implication was clear: I was an exceptionally sorry specimen on display, an outlier in the herd. I turned to the audience and asked, "Have any of you ever been wounded by humanity?" They laughed with me; in that moment, we knew that we were all weird, all in this together, and that addressing our own suffering while learning not to inflict it on others is part of the work we're all here to do. So is love, which comes in so many forms and can be directed at so many things. There are many questions in life worth asking, but perhaps if we're wise we can understand that not every question needs an answer.

1.
Silence Is Broken

A Short History
of Silence

*"What I most regretted were my silences. . . . And there are so
many silences to be broken."*

—Audre Lorde

THE OCEAN AROUND THE ARCHIPELAGO

Silence is golden, or so I was told when I was young. Later, everything changed. Silence equals death, the queer activists fighting
the neglect and repression around AIDS shouted in the streets.
Silence is the ocean of the unsaid, the unspeakable, the repressed,
the erased, the unheard. It surrounds the scattered islands made up
of those allowed to speak and of what can be said and who listens.
Silence occurs in many ways for many reasons; each of us has his or
her own sea of unspoken words.

English is full of overlapping words, but for the purposes of
this essay, regard *silence* as what is imposed and *quiet* as what is
sought. The tranquility of a quiet place, of quieting one's own mind,
of a retreat from words and bustle, is acoustically the same as the
silence of intimidation or repression but psychically and politically
something entirely different. What is unsaid because serenity and
introspection are sought is as different from what is not said be-

cause the threats are high or the barriers are great as swimming is from drowning. Quiet is to noise as silence is to communication. The quiet of the listener makes room for the speech of others, like the quiet of the reader taking in words on the page, like the white of the paper taking ink.

"We are volcanoes," Ursula K. Le Guin once remarked. "When we women offer our experience as our truth, as human truth, all the maps change. There are new mountains." The new voices that are undersea volcanoes erupt in open water, and new islands are born; it's a furious business and a startling one. The world changes. Silence is what allows people to suffer without recourse, what allows hypocrisies and lies to grow and flourish, crimes to go unpunished. If our voices are essential aspects of our humanity, to be rendered voiceless is to be dehumanized or excluded from one's humanity. And the history of silence is central to women's history.

Words bring us together, and silence separates us, leaves us bereft of the help or solidarity or just communion that speech can solicit or elicit. Some species of trees spread root systems underground that interconnect the individual trunks and weave the individual trees into a more stable whole that can't so easily be blown down in the wind. Stories and conversations are like those roots. For a century, the human response to stress and danger has been defined as "fight or flight." A 2000 UCLA study by several psychologists noted that this research was based largely on studies of male rats and male human beings. But studying women led them to a third, often deployed option: gather for solidarity, support, advice. They noted that "behaviorally, females' responses are more marked by a pattern of 'tend-and-befriend.' Tending involves nurturant activities designed to protect the self and offspring that promote safety and reduce distress; befriending is the creation and maintenance of social networks that may aid in this process." Much of this is done through speech, through telling of one's plight, through being heard, through hearing compassion and understanding in the response of the people you tend to, whom you befriend. Not only women do this, but perhaps women do this more routinely. It's how I cope, or how my community helps me cope, now that I have one.

Being unable to tell your story is a living death and sometimes a literal one. If no one listens when you say your ex-husband is trying to kill you, if no one believes you when you say you are in pain, if no one hears you when you say *help*, if you don't dare say *help*, if you have been trained not to bother people by saying *help*. If you are considered to be out of line when you speak up in a meeting, are not admitted into an institution of power, are subject to irrelevant criticism whose subtext is that women should not be here, or heard. Stories save your life. And stories are your life. We are our stories, stories that can be both prison and the crowbar to break open the door of that prison; we make stories to save ourselves or to trap ourselves or others, stories that lift us up or smash us against the stone wall of our own limits and fears. Liberation is always in part a storytelling process: breaking stories, breaking silences, making new stories. A free person tells her own story. A valued person lives in a society in which her story has a place.

Violence against women is often against our voices and our stories. It is a refusal of our voices, and of what a voice means: the right to self-determination, to participation, to consent or dissent, to live and participate, to interpret and narrate. A husband hits his wife to silence her; a date rapist or acquaintance rapist refuses to let the "no" of his victim mean what it should, that she alone has jurisdiction over her body; rape culture asserts that women's testimony is worthless, untrustworthy; anti-abortion activists also seek to silence the self-determination of women; a murderer silences forever. These are assertions that the victim has no rights, no value, is not an equal. These silencings take place in smaller ways: the people harassed and badgered into silence online, talked over and cut out in conversation, belittled, humiliated, dismissed. Having a voice is crucial. It's not all there is to human rights, but it's central to them, and so you can consider the history of women's rights and lack of rights as a history of silence and breaking silence.

Speech, words, voice sometimes change things in themselves when they bring about inclusion, recognition, the rehumanization that undoes dehumanization. Sometimes they are only the preconditions to changing rules, laws, regimes to bring about justice and liberty. Sometimes just being able to speak, to be heard, to be believed are crucial parts of membership in a family, a community, a society. Sometimes our voices break those things apart; sometimes those things are prisons. And then when words break through unspeakability, what was tolerated by a society sometimes becomes intolerable. Those not impacted can fail to see or feel the impact of segregation or police brutality or domestic violence: stories bring home the trouble and make it unavoidable.

By *voice*, I don't mean only literal voice—the sound produced by the vocal cords in the ears of others—but the ability to speak up, to participate, to experience oneself and be experienced as a free person with rights. This includes the right not to speak, whether it's the right against being tortured to confess, as political prisoners are, or not to be expected to service strangers who approach you, as some men do to young women, demanding attention and flattery and punishing their absence. The idea of voice expanded to the idea of agency includes wide realms of power and powerlessness.*

---

* Once, talking to cultural historian Joel Dinerstein while he was researching his *American Cool* project, I asked why there were so few women on the list, and then I realized that the refusal to reach out or react that is the essence of much masculine cool would too often be read as catatonia or unacceptable arrogance from a woman. What makes him cool makes her cold.

Who has been unheard? The sea is vast, and the surface of the ocean is unmappable. We know who has, mostly, been heard on the official subjects: who held office, attended university, commanded armies, served as judges and juries, wrote books, and ran empires over the past several centuries. We know how it has changed some-what, thanks to the countless revolutions of the twentieth century and after—against colonialism, against racism, against misogyny, against the innumerable enforced silences homophobia imposed, and so much more. We know that in the United States class was leveled out to some extent in the twentieth century and then rein-forced toward the end, through income inequality and the with-ering away of social mobility and the rise of a new extreme elite. Poverty silences.

Who has been heard we know; they are the well-mapped is-lands, the rest are the unmappable sea of unheard, unrecorded hu-manity. Many over the centuries were heard and loved, and their words disappeared in the air as soon as they were spoken but took root in minds, contributed to the culture, like something com-posting into rich earth; new things grew from those words. Many others were silenced, excluded, ignored. The earth is seven-tenths water, but the ratio of silence to voice is far greater. If libraries hold all the stories that have been told, there are ghost libraries of all the stories that have not. The ghosts outnumber the books by some unimaginably vast sum. Even those who have been audible have often earned the privilege through strategic silences or the inability to hear certain voices, including their own.

The struggle of liberation has been in part to create the conditions for the formerly silenced to speak and be heard. An Englishwoman tells me that Britain has a growing prison population of old men, because countless victims whom no one was willing to hear before are now telling of sexual abuse. The most notorious British case is of

BBC entertainer Jimmy Savile, who was knighted and lauded and made into a celebrity. He died before more than 450 people charged him with sexual abuse, mostly young women but also younger boys and adult women. Four hundred and fifty people who were not heard, who perhaps did not think they had the right to speak out or even to object or to be believed. Or rather knew that they lacked those rights, that they were the voiceless.

John Lydon, aka Johnny Rotten of the Sex Pistols, said to the BBC of Savile, in 1978, "I bet he's into all kinds of seediness that we all know about, but are not allowed to talk about. I know some rumors. I bet none of this will be allowed out." Lydon's words weren't allowed out until 2013, when the unedited interview was released. Around that time other stories surfaced of pedophile rings involving prominent British politicians. Many of the crimes had happened long before. Some reportedly resulted in the deaths of child victims. Scandals involving public figures provide national and international versions of what are otherwise often small, local dramas about whose story will prevail. They are often how the winds of opinion change, as they prompt conversations. Sometimes they lay the groundwork for others to come forward to speak of other damage and other perpetrators. Lately, this has evolved into a process using social media to create collective tribunals, mass testimony, and mutual support that could be seen as a version of that "tend-and-befriend" behavior outlined above.

Silence is what allowed predators to rampage through the decades, unchecked. It's as though the voices of these prominent public men devoured the voices of others into nothingness, a narrative cannibalism. They rendered them voiceless to refuse and afflicted with unbelievable stories. *Unbelievable* means those with power did not want to know, to hear, to believe, did not want them to have voices. People died from being unheard. Then something changed.

The same story could be told of innumerable North American figures, of whom the famous recent examples are Fox News CEO Roger Ailes, charged by several women with workplace sexual harassment and persecution, exploitation, blackmail, and psychological abuse over a half century; Bill Cosby and his serial drug-aided rapes over the same time span; and Jian Ghomeshi in Canada, charged by several women with brutal assaults—powerful figures who knew their voices and credibility could drown out those they assaulted, until something broke, until silence was broken, until an ocean of stories roared forth and washed away their impunity. Even when the evidence was overwhelming some still hurled abuse and threats at the victims and found ways to deny the merits of their stories. Because to believe them would mean questioning foundational assumptions. It would be uncomfortable, and many speak of comfort as a right, even when—especially when—that comfort is built upon the suffering and silencing of others.

If the right to speak, if having credibility, if being heard is a kind of wealth, that wealth is now being redistributed. There has long been an elite with audibility and credibility, an underclass of the voiceless. As the wealth is redistributed, the stunned incomprehension of the elites erupts over and over again, a fury and disbelief that this woman or child dared to speak up, that people deigned to believe her, that her voice counts for something, that her truth may end a powerful man's reign. These voices, heard, upend power relations. A hotel cleaning woman launched the beginning of the end of International Monetary Fund chief and serial assailant Dominique Strauss-Kahn's career. Women have ended the careers of stars in many fields—or rather those stars have destroyed themselves by acts they engaged in with the belief that they had the impunity that comes with their victims' powerlessness. Many had impunity for many years, some for lifetimes; many now have found they no longer do.

Who is heard and who is not defines the status quo. Those who embody it, often at the cost of extraordinary silences with themselves, move to the center; those who embody what is not heard or what violates those who rise on silence are cast out. By redefining whose voice is valued, we redefine our society and its values.

My subject in this book is that subspecies of silence and silencing specific to women, if anything can be specific to more than half of humanity. If to have a voice, to be allowed to speak, to be heard and believed is essential to being an insider or a person of power, a human being with full membership, then it's important to recognize that silence is the universal condition of oppression, and there are many kinds of silence and of the silenced.

The category *women* is a long boulevard that intersects with many other avenues, including class, race, poverty and wealth. Traveling this boulevard means crossing others, and it never means that the city of silence has only one street or one route through it that matters. It is now useful to question the categories of male and female, but it's also useful to remember that misogyny is based on a devout belief in the reality of those categories (or is an attempt to reinforce them by demonstrating the proper role of each gender).

Genocide is a great silencing, and so is slavery. And it was in opposition to slavery that American feminism arose, born at the intersection. Elizabeth Cady Stanton went to the World's Antislavery Convention in London in 1840, one of many women abolitionists who traveled to participate, only to find that they could not be seated and could not speak. Even people who considered themselves champions of the oppressed could not see what was oppressive about an order so old it was perceived as natural. A controversy arose. Stanton wrote in her autobiography of the remarkable women gathered there, who were "all compelled to listen in silence to the masculine platitudes on women's sphere." She went home furious, and that fury at being silenced and shut out, and the insight that resulted, gave rise to the first women's rights movement.

Along with gaining voting rights and access to schools and education, a significant part of the civil rights struggle was—and is—to include people of color on juries, both to give them the right of full participation and to give people on trial the right to be heard by people who might have some understanding of who they are and where they came from—a jury of their peers, as guaranteed in the Constitution. The racial makeup of juries was still being contested in the Supreme Court in 2016. The struggles around gender are analogous.

In 1927, seven years after women gained the vote nationally,[†] only nineteen states allowed women to serve on juries, and, even in 1961, the Supreme Court upheld Florida's automatic exemption of women jurors. Which means that many, many trials for gender violence and discrimination were heard by all-male juries in courtrooms with male lawyers presided over by male judges, a setup in which a woman victim's voice was extraordinarily likely to be discredited and silenced (unless she was testifying against someone in another silenced group: white women were sometimes used by white men as weapons against Black men). And that in this as in so many other ways, women did not have a voice in their society.

---

† It's sometimes said that Black women didn't get the vote until the civil rights era, which is true for both Black women and Black men in much of the South, but not of the nation as a whole; Black women in Chicago were organizing voting blocs before 1920, because Illinois women won the vote in 1913. Four Western states—Wyoming, Utah, Colorado, and Idaho—gave women the vote in the nineteenth century. Asian and Native women were disenfranchised in other ways well into the twentieth century, and some white women in the suffrage movement denigrated and excluded Black women. After the Civil War, founding feminist Elizabeth Cady Stanton did not want to support the right of Black men to vote as an issue separate from the right of women to vote, which meant she and a sector of the women's movement did not support this struggle or even actively opposed it. Racist voter disenfranchisement became a major issue again in the twenty-first century.

Silence was the historic condition of women, denied education and a role in public life—positions as judges, priests, or almost any other speaking role—with rare exceptions. Women were silent in the houses of the spirit. In I Corinthians, St. Paul ordered, "Let your women keep silence in the churches: for it is not permitted unto them to speak." Elsewhere the New Testament declares, "But I suffer not a woman to teach, nor to usurp authority over the man, but to be in silence." No woman became a priest in the Anglican Church in the United States until 1944, none in the Church of England until 1994. The first woman rabbi in the United States was ordained in 1972. No woman has been ordained in the Catholic Church.

Women were silent in the courts. No woman served on the US Supreme Court until 1981, and women currently only hold a third of the seats, the most ever. At Harvard Law School, where so many of the lords of the earth were groomed, the first petition for a woman's admittance was in 1871, and the first woman entered in 1950. Women were excluded from undergraduate enrollment in many of the Ivy League universities, where global power alliances are formed. The first woman undergraduate at Yale entered in 1969. The reception women received there was so hostile that in 1977 the nation's first Title IX lawsuit for campus sexual harassment and rape by professors, *Alexander v. Yale,* was filed. It set a precedent requiring campuses across the country to address these abuses as discrimination (but not enough changed: thirty-nine years later, in the summer of 2016, 169 philosophers signed a letter decrying a twenty-seven-year series of alleged sexual harassment incidents by Yale professor Thomas Pogge, whose specialty is the field of ethics).

New recognitions required new language, and feminism coined a plethora of words to describe the individual experiences that the conversations of the 1960s and 1970s were beginning to flush out of hiding. Susan Brownmiller coined the term *date rape* in 1975. The term *sexual harassment* was perhaps coined in 1974 by Mary Rowe to describe misconduct at MIT, or by a group of women addressing the same problem at Cornell in 1975. The legendary lawyer Catherine MacKinnnon took the concept forward with her 1979 book *Sexual Harassment of Working Women*. The term and the concepts behind it would only become well known to the public with the Clarence Thomas–Anita Hill hearings in 1991. In 1993, Oklahoma and North Carolina became the last states to make raping one's spouse a crime. Lack of jurisdiction over one's own body is a form of silencing, a way of making what one says have no value, and words without value are worse than silence: one can be punished for them.

II: EVERY MAN AN ISLAND: MALE SILENCE

Silence is present everywhere under patriarchy, though it requires different silences from men than from women. You can imagine the policing of gender as the creation of reciprocal silences, and you can begin to recognize male silence as a tradeoff for power and membership. No one ever put it better than bell hooks, who said:

> The first act of violence that patriarchy demands of males is not violence toward women. Instead patriarchy demands of all males that they engage in acts of psychic self-mutilation, that they kill off the emotional parts of themselves. If an individual is not successful in emotionally crippling himself, he can count on patriarchal men to enact rituals of power that will assault his self-esteem.

That is, patriarchy requires that men silence themselves first (and perhaps it's worth noting again that, though patriarchy is a system that privileges men and masculinity, many women are complicit in it, some men rebel against it, and some people are undoing the rules of gender that prop it up). This means learning not only to be silent to others but also to themselves, about aspects of their inner life and self.

Reading hooks's passage, I was chilled, as though I suddenly understood that this is the plot of a horror movie or a zombie movie. The deadened seek out the living to exterminate feeling, either by making their targets join them in numbness or by intimidating or assaulting them into silence. In the landscape of silence, the three realms might be silence imposed from within; silence imposed from without; and silence that exists around what has not yet been named, recognized, described, or admitted. But they are not distinct; they feed each other; and what is unsayable becomes unknowable and vice versa, until something breaks.

A certain kind of emotional wholeness is the price men pay for power, and the renunciations begin early. When I questioned a nephew, as neutrally as possible, just before he turned five, about why pink was no longer among his favorite colors, he knew exactly what we were talking about: "I like girls. I just don't like girl *things*," he exclaimed, and he knew what girl things were and that he must not let them define him. In fact, he already despised them and segued into a tirade against My Little Pony.

I thought five was early to be bombarded until I shopped for a friend's unborn son and was reminded that our roles seize us at birth. Girls get being cuddly, pretty, attractive, and maybe passive: warm colors, kittens and flowers and flourishes. Boys get distance: cool colors and active figures, often menacing ones or ones that are removed from intimacy and emotion—sports figures, balls and bats, rocket ships, cold-blooded animals like reptiles, dinosaurs, and sharks, strange choices for helpless mammals who depend on nurture.

Masculinity is a great renunciation. The color pink is a small thing, but emotions, expressiveness, receptiveness, a whole array of possibilities get renounced by successful boys and men in everyday life, and often for men who inhabit masculinized realms—

sports, the military, the police, all-male workforces in construction or resource extraction—even more must be renounced to belong. Women get to keep a wider range of emotional possibility, though they are discouraged or stigmatized for expressing some of the fiercer ones, the feelings that aren't ladylike and deferential, and so much else—ambition, critical intelligence, independent analysis, dissent, anger. That is to say, silence is a pervasive force, distributed differently to different categories of people. It underlies a status quo that depends upon a homeostasis of silences.

Misogyny and homophobia are both forms of hating that which is not patriarchy. "What causes heterosexuality?" asked one of the stickers put up around my hometown as part of Queer Nation's insurgent campaign against homophobia a quarter century ago. It was a brilliant question reversing the conventional one, recognizing that heterosexuality was also socially constructed and did not have to be regarded as an unquestionable norm. I've been blessed to be around gay men since I was thirteen, around people who have resisted the indoctrinations of heterosexual masculinity, since at least some of its privileges excluded them or didn't interest them or weren't worth the tradeoff to them, or because dissenting erotically opened up the possibility of other kinds of dissent. Knowing them has been a long encounter with what else men could be.

Many of the gay men in my life have seemed more whole than most of the straight men I've known. They have been more able to experience and express a full range of emotion and to understand and appreciate it in others (and often to have honed perception of nuances and shades of meaning beyond the rest of us as well as the wit to express it). They have been soldiers who defected from patriarchy's war, people with the binocular vision we call humor: the ability to recognize the gaps between how things are and how they are supposed to be.

Masculinity itself was and is open to question in a culture that includes the spectrum from drag queens to aestheticized hyper-masculinity, and in which men recognized themselves as subject of the male gaze. Beneath it all lies a sense that all identities are a costume you don, and behind that lies latitude about who you want to be. Of course everyone in every category of human being has the right to be awful, and the mere fact of one's orientation, like one's race, class, religion, and gender, doesn't necessarily generate liberation or insight; I am speaking not of all gay men but of my own friends and community.

In the heterosexual mainstream, women have performed the labor of holding and expressing emotion for others. When I was very young, I went on a road trip with my boyfriend, whose father, seeing us off, said, "Keep in touch. Your mother will be worried." She was the stand-in for his inexpressible emotions. She had the feelings that could be acknowledged. She was the one who filled in the home's silence with chatter to try to keep people connected, to be open in a house full of kind but shut-down men, decent men who were at worst uncomfortable with emotional expression and felt that connection was not their work.

If emotion must be killed, this is work that can make women targets. Less decent men hunt out vulnerability, because if being a man means learning to hate vulnerability, then you hate it in yourself and in the gender that has been carrying it for you. *Girl* and *pussy* have long been key insults used against boys and men, along with *gay* and *faggot*; a man must not be a woman, must not cry, must not be weak; and the fear of being gay was of being sexual in some way that might not be about domination and penetration, might be about being penetrated, being equal, being open. As if openness were weakness rather than strength. In ancient Greece and some contemporary cultures, masculinity has been defined by being he who penetrates. Being he or she who is penetrated is regarded as degradation equivalent to not being masculine—which makes being heterosexually female a perpetual state of degradation and, perhaps, equates the penetrator to he who degrades. (In medieval Iceland, the insult "a troll uses you like a woman" was considered so deadly that the insulted party was granted the legal right to kill.)

Love is a constant negotiation, a constant conversation; to love someone is to lay yourself open to rejection and abandonment; love is something you can earn but not extort. It is an arena in which you are not in control, because someone else also has rights and decisions; it is a collaborative process; making love is at its best a process in which those negotiations become joy and play. So much sexual violence is a refusal of that vulnerability; so many of the instructions about masculinity inculcate a lack of skills and willingness to negotiate in good faith. Inability and entitlement deteriorate into a rage to control, to turn a conversation into a monologue of commands, to turn the collaboration of making love into the imposition of assault and the assertion of control. Rape is hate and fury taking love's place between bodies. It's a vision of the male body as a weapon and the female body (in heterosexual rape) as the enemy. What is it like to weaponize your body?

If you have not been taught to collaborate, to negotiate, to respect and pay attention, if you do not regard the beloved as your equal, endowed with certain inalienable rights, you are not well equipped for the work of love. We are in a world where men until recently in the industrialized world assumed that access to women's bodies was a right that women should not impede. It's still common to hear heterosexual men complain of the onerous unreasonableness of having to earn sexual access, and maybe we should remember that until recently in the United States husbands had unrestricted rights to their wives' bodies, which is the other way to say that wives had almost no rights over their own bodies.

Only in California and New York in recent years did affirmative consent become the statewide standard for consensual sex on college campuses. When affirmative consent was signed into law, a host of men in the United States (and on the London-based *Guardian*'s website) raised a shriek of indignation that both parties had to be consciously, actively in favor of what was going on. It was telling that they regarded this as a terrible obstacle, newly erected. The previous criterion had been the absence of dissent, which of course meant intimidation, intoxication, and unconsciousness could all be read as consent. Silence was consent, in other words, as though silence said one thing when it can say so many, as though the burden was to issue a *no* rather than elicit a *yes*.

It's traditional to separate out rape from domestic violence from murder from institutional misogyny. But women being raped and beaten and harassed on the street and stalked often fear, with good reason, that they are also going to be killed, and sometimes they—we—are. The distinctions between the kinds of violence don't serve us when they prevent us from talking about what gets called *gender violence* as a broad and deep phenomenon. And that even calling it all gender violence obscures that violence is only a means to an end, and that there are other means as well. If the subject is silence, then how some silence others broadens the query into one that can include shame, humiliation, exclusion, devaluation, discrediting, threats, and the unequal distribution of power through social, economic, cultural, and legal means.

Domestic violence expert Evan Stark argues that the very term is wrong; he writes in his 2009 book *Coercive Control: How Men Entrap Women in Personal Life,*

This book reframes woman battering from the standpoint of its survivors as a course of calculated, malevolent conduct deployed almost exclusively by men to dominate individual women by interweaving repeated physical abuse with three equally important tactics: intimidation, isolation, and control. . . . The primary harm abusive men inflict is political, not physical, and reflects the deprivation of rights and resources that are critical to personhood and citizenship.

He compares it to kidnapping, its victims to hostages, often cut off from access to other people, to freedom of movement, to material resources such as money or cars, punished for infractions by the dictator of the household. Often the most dangerous time is when victims of coercive control try to leave. Many are killed for trying, or for succeeding in reaching freedom, a freedom that is not safety. Stark adds,

The women in my practice have repeatedly made clear that what is done to them is less important than what their partners have prevented them from doing for themselves by appropriating their resources; undermining their social support; subverting their rights to privacy, self-respect, and autonomy; and depriving them of substantial equality. . . . Coercive control is a liberty crime rather than a crime of assault.

The actress and feminist activist Patricia Arquette noted in 2016,

There's a ripple effect in being underpaid for women. Ten thousand women are turned down every day for domestic abuse shelters. Part of domestic abuse is often economic suppression; the male might take your paycheck every week and never give you money or allow you to work because he's too jealous. The number-one reason women say they returned to their abuser is financial insecurity. Often they have kids with them.

We can expand on Stark's framework to see many forms of attack on women—by strangers and acquaintances, by politicians and the state, not just by intimate partners—as coercive control. The endless war against reproductive rights—against not only abortion but also birth control and access to family planning and sex education—is an attempt at institutional coercive control. Violence sometimes plays a role, but coercion occurs by many other means, including the making of punitive and rights-denying laws. It's not hard to see legislation that pretends to focus on the rights of the unborn over the rights of women in whom the unborn are situated as actually focused on the rights of men and the state over women's bodies; or to see, in the effort to deny access to birth control and abortion, an attack on women's autonomy, agency, and right to choose what sex means to them, to control their own bodies, to pursue pleasure and connection without submitting to the enormous demands of maternity, or to choose that maternity on their own terms.

The widespread existence of gender violence and sexual violence serves to curtail the freedom and confidence of those who must navigate in a world where threats become a background element to their lives, a footnote on every page, a cloud in every sky. These are not "crimes of passion," as they were often called, or of desire, but of the fury to control and to reinforce or reimpose the power structure. A lot of domestic violence homicides are punishment for or attempts to continue controlling women who have announced they are leaving, tried to leave, or left. Killing someone is killing her freedom, her autonomy, her power, her voice. That many men believe they have the right and the need to control women, violently or otherwise, says much about the belief systems they inhabit, about the culture we exist within.

In recent years, from Brazil to Canada, rapists have filmed their sexual assaults. The video is then circulated among male peers as evidence of the agency of the rapists and the lack of agency of the victim, the subsequent humiliation and loss of control over her privacy and dignity (and much mainstream heterosexual porn reiterates this scenario in endless variations, with excitement seeming to come from homoerotic power, not heterosexual pleasure). This shaming drives some rape survivors to suicide—and it says a lot that a sexual assault is supposed to be shameful for the victim and not the perpetrator. These videos remind us of the coexistence of two wildly different worlds: when they circulate in the legal system, they are evidence of crimes, but when they circulate in the perpetrators' peer group, they demonstrate to the others the perpetrators' conformity to norms of masculinity.

But the law and the rapists are not so different in other ways. Many rape cases bring victims into court or university proceedings where the administrators perpetuate the discrediting and devaluing of the victim with questions that treat her like a perpetrator, cast her as an inherently untrustworthy person, attack her with intrusive, irrelevant, and prurient questions, often about her sexual history. University and legal authorities sometimes express more concern over the future of campus rapists than that of their victims and are often more inclined to grant credibility to the former than the latter. The consequent unwillingness of many survivors to cooperate with the legal system results in a loss of their legal rights, in silencing, in allowing rapists to go unpunished and often to act again, and in a society (the United States) in which only 3 percent of rapists serve time for their crimes.

Thus does coercive control happen at a societal level as it does in the home. Women are instructed, by the way victims are treated and by the widespread tolerance of an epidemic of violence, that their value is low, that speaking up may result in more punishment, that silence may be a better survival strategy. Sometimes this is called *rape culture*, but like *domestic violence*, the term narrows the focus to one act rather than the motive for many; *patriarchy* is a more useful overarching term.

The pandemic of campus rape reminds us that this particular kind of crime is not committed by a group that can be dismissed as marginal in any way; fraternities at elite institutions from Vanderbilt to Stanford have been the scenes of extraordinarily vicious acts; every spring the finest universities graduate a new crop of unpunished rapists. They remind us that this deadness is at the heart of things, not the margins, that failure of empathy and respect are central, not marginal.

Empathy is a narrative we tell ourselves to make other people real to us, to feel for and with them, and thereby to extend and enlarge and open ourselves. To be without empathy is to have shut down or killed off some part of yourself and your humanity, to have protected yourself from some kind of vulnerability. Silencing, or refusing to hear, breaks this social contract of recognizing another's humanity and our connectedness.

Contemplating a book of lynching photographs published a few decades ago, I imagined the white people who brought their children and picnics to the torture scenes were celebrating their numbness, their separation. The people making or consuming rape videos and misogynist porn must be doing the same. Our humanity is made out of stories or, in the absence of words and narratives, out of imagination: that which I did not literally feel, because it happened to you and not to me, I can imagine as though it were me, or care about it though it was not me. Thus we are connected, thus we are not separate. Those stories can be killed into silence, and the voices that might breed empathy silenced, discredited, censored, rendered unspeakable, unhearable. Discrimination is training in not identifying or empathizing with someone because they are different in some way, in believing the differences mean everything and common humanity nothing.

In his book *Love and War: How Militarism Shapes Sexuality and*

Romance, Tom Digby argues that ours is a militarized society in which men are pressured in a thousand ways to take on the mores and skills of soldiers. A soldier surrounded by the deaths of others and the possibility of his own mangling and death shuts down. So do many survivors of atrocities, individual and collective, atrocities often committed by those who shut down in order to perpetrate atrocities. Robert Jay Lifton described this emotional numbness as *Death in Life*, the title of his book on Hiroshima survivors. He argues that they survived the horror by shutting down, but that remaining shut down meant being the walking dead, the unalive. This brings us back to hooks's critique of men's "acts of psychic self-mutilation." Maybe the question is what it means to be alive, and how to be fully alive.

Soldiers are trained to wither away empathy in order to make them killing machines; it dispatches them to do their work in war; it sends them home with trauma that is itself often unspeakable. David Morris, in *The Evil Hours*, his remarkable book on trauma, notes, "Part of trauma's corrosive power lies in its ability to destroy narrative, and . . . stories, written and spoken, have tremendous healing power for both the teller and the listener. Normal, nontraumatic memories are owned and integrated into the ongoing story of the self. These are, in a sense, like domesticated animals, amenable to control, tractable. In contrast, the traumatic memory stands apart, like a feral dog, snarling, wild, and unpredictable."

Morris notes that rape victims and soldiers have much in common. Trauma disrupts the narrative of a life because it shatters memory into shards that will not be recognized as a credible story, sometimes even by the teller—thus some survivors of rape and other atrocities emerge with fractured stories that are seen as signs of their unbelievability, unreliability, untrustworthiness. Thus rape is an act that seeks to shatter the self and its narrative, sometimes followed by legal proceedings that require the self to reassemble as a coherent narrative (but not too coherent: successful testimony must be neither too clinically cool nor too emotionally overloaded). A friend who works in the field says that many women report sexual assault for altruistic reasons: to prevent it from happening to someone else. Sometimes they come forward to support the testimony of someone who's spoken out first. Speaking up is, in other words, often an act of empathy.

Morris continues, "Despite the fact that rape is the most common and most injurious form of trauma, the bulk of PTSD research is directed toward war trauma and veterans. Most of what we know about PTSD comes from studying men." There is, in other words, a silence about who suffers this affliction that further silences women. Silences build atop silences, a city of silence that wars against stories. A host of citizens silencing themselves to be accepted by the silenced. People meeting as caricatures of human beings, offering their silence to each other, their ability to avoid connection. Dams and seawalls built against the stories, which sometimes break through and flood the city.

III: SILENCE: THE CAGES

There are those who are literally silent.

"Who, if I cried out, would hear me," begins Rainer Maria Rilke's first *Duino Elegy*, and there are those who hear no one, not even themselves, who have repressed, forgotten, buried the knowledge and thereby buried themselves. When we look for silence we constantly find the dead. Who would hear them? Only people who would punish them further. Sarah Chang wrote of watching child pornography as part of her job as a prosecutor of sexual abuse crimes against children. She noted their silence.

In video after video, I witnessed silent suffering. I later learned that this is a typical reaction of young abuse victims. Psychiatrists say the silence conveys their sense of helplessness, which also manifests as a reluctance to report the incidents and their tendency to accommodate their abusers. If children do disclose their abuse, their reports are often ambivalent, sometimes followed by a complete retraction and a return to silence.

She speaks of one victim whose brother threatened to kill her if she screamed. Maya Angelou was mute for five years after she was raped, at age seven.

In his childhood, Barry Lopez was raped repeatedly over a period of years by a family friend. He writes of his rapist,

> He told me, calmly but emphatically, that he was a doctor, that I needed treatment, and that we were not going to be adding to Mother's worries by telling her about my problem. From time to time, often on the drive back to my home, Shier would remind me that if I were ever to tell anyone, if the treatments were to stop, he would have no choice but to have me committed to an institution. . . . It would be best, I thought, if I just continued to be the brave boy he said I was.

He was silenced for years, and when he spoke up in his mid-teens, his stepfather wavered and then decided not to believe him. Half a century passed before he spoke publicly of his ordeal and its traumas.

When the mouth may not speak, the body sometimes reveals: silent testimony.

Kelly Sundberg wrote about her violent ex-husband and her shifting relationship to that violence:

> Two years after we moved, I started graduate school and finally made some friends, but it was hard to spend time with them. I had to lie: I shut my arm in the door. I tripped on a rug and hit my face on the table. I don't know where that bruise came from. I

think I did it in my sleep. I think I'm anemic. I just bruise so easily.

Once, Caleb said to me, "You probably wish that someone would figure out where those bruises are coming from. You probably wish someone knew, so that things could change." He said it with such sadness.

He only hit me in the face once. A red bruise bloomed across my cheek, and my eye was split and oozing. Afterwards, we both sat on the bathroom floor, exhausted. "You made me hit you in the face," he said mournfully. "Now everyone is going to know."

She had been silent. But her face told. The truth was a menace to her husband, her marriage, the comfort and assumptions of those around her. Sundberg broke the silence and wrote about it in a widely acclaimed essay that served as an invitation to others to tell their own stories about violence from spouses and parents. A solo voice became a chorus.

One disturbing aspect of abuse and harassment is the idea that it's not the crime that's the betrayal but the testimony about the crime. You're not supposed to tell. Abusers often assume this privilege that demands the silence of the abused, that a nonreciprocal protection be in place. Others often impose it as well, portraying the victims as choosing to ruin a career or a family, as though the assailant did not make that choice himself.

There are voices raised in the absence of listeners.

In 2015, a Stanford University student sexually assaulted an unconscious woman. The woman testified at his trial, "I tried to push it out of my mind, but it was so heavy I didn't talk, I didn't eat, I didn't sleep, I didn't interact with anyone. After work, I would drive to a secluded place to scream. . . ." She had somehow absorbed the idea that her trauma and fury did not belong, that her screams should not be heard. But then she was heard around the world. She wrote a letter to her assailant that, after she read it aloud in court and it was entered in the court record, became, in June 2016, perhaps the most widely viewed first-person account of rape and its aftermath ever. She regained the voice taken away from her and with it rehumanized her dehumanized self. She spoke words that built a cage around him, erected a monument to his casual malice, words that will likely follow him all his life. Her voice was her power.

She broke the silence (though she didn't break the shame and fear that often keeps rape victims anonymous). She spoke of him and his evasions and lies with fury and outrage, but she ended with tenderness: "To girls everywhere, I am with you. On nights when you feel alone, I am with you. When people doubt or dismiss you, I am with you. I fought every day for you. So never stop fighting, I believe you. . . . you can't be silenced." *I am with you* is the voice of empathy, the words that say we are not separate from each other.

But there are those who scream in vain.

The famous case of Kitty Genovese, raped and stabbed to death by a stranger, while people in the surrounding apartments ignored her screams, was turned into a mythic example of bystander indifference. Catherine Pelonero revisited the case in 2014. In a review of her book, Peter C. Baker pointed out:

> The same month that Genovese was murdered, Pelonero points out, United Press International ran a story about a judge in Cleveland who had ruled that "it's all right for a husband to give his wife a black eye and knock out one of her teeth if she stays out too late." Pelonero also quotes more extensively the many witnesses who explicitly justified their inaction in terms of expectations about women and their place in the world. "I figured it was a lovers' quarrel, that her man had knocked her down. So my wife and I went back to bed."

Baker comments,

> The story was retold again and again by college professors and pundits, almost always in such a way that it was never specifically about violence against women, or the complex latticework of legal and cultural arrangements that allows such violence to flourish. Instead, it became a classic tale of human "nature"—and like most such tales, it has almost nothing to say about the fine grain of human practice or experience.

In other words, the story was noise filled with silence about the real causes of Genovese's death and that of many other women.

Along with those who are accused of lying, imagining, making things up out of malice, confusion, or madness, there are people who are believed but told their suffering and rights are of no consequence.
Many years before, my mother had approached a policeman to tell him that her husband, my father, was beating her. The officer gave her some platitudinous advice—I think it was about cooking nice dinners—and made it clear that this was one kind of assault to which the law was indifferent. There was no use to speaking up. In her 1976 book on domestic violence, when the silence around the subject was just being broken, the great lesbian-rights activist Del Martin wrote, "These women bear the brutality of their husband in silence because they have no one to turn to and nowhere to go."‡ Feminism changed the laws. But turning to the police, who have their own high incidence of domestic violence and limited tools to make restraining orders mean anything, is a strategy that often fails.

‡ Martin, in 1955 a cofounder of the Daughters of Bilitis, the nation's first lesbian-rights group, married her partner of fifty-one years, Phyllis Lyon, in February 2004 in the first of San Francisco's season of same-sex weddings that launched the momentum for marriage equality that culminated in the Supreme Court's 2015 decision.

There are people who speak and are believed, and the consequence is that they disappear.

There is somewhere to go in many communities, the secret sanctuaries that are women's shelters, places into which women disappear as a result of violence, losing their home and quite literally their place in the world as a result of their partner's violence. Many women are refugees in their own country; many women are forced to disappear from their own homes and lives and take up secret lives in secret locations. *Battered women's shelters*, as they were then called, sprang up in the 1970s. They exist by the thousands in North America and Britain, if not on a scale to receive all the victims of domestic violence. My mother volunteered at one for years after her divorce. She did the accounting.

And there are people who speak up and are silenced under the law.

"The Little Mermaid" is a story written by Hans Christian Andersen, a man who was queer in many senses, the awkward, immense, sexually ambiguous illegitimate son of a peasant woman, who became the darling of aristocrats. It is a tale of how a mermaid trades her voice for a chance at life on earth. She comes out of the sea with legs, without words. Like the silenced heroine of Andersen's "The Wild Swans," she must not, she cannot advocate for herself. In 2011, when Nafissatou Diallo, a room cleaner at an upscale hotel in Manhattan, was sexually assaulted by the head of the International Monetary Fund, Dominique Strauss-Kahn, she was vilified and discredited in the media, and the prosecutors backed down from the case, but she won a civil suit against Strauss-Kahn. The price, as with so many of these cases, was silence.

The Center for Public Integrity reported in 2009, "But while the vast majority of students who are sexually assaulted remain silent—just over 95 percent, according to a study funded by the research arm of the U.S. Justice Department—those who come forward can encounter mystifying disciplinary proceedings, secretive school administrations, and off-the-record negotiations." At the University of Virginia, accusers were told that they had to remain silent about all aspects of their cases and risked penalties for disobedience, until the federal government intervened. And Buzzfeed reported in 2015, "A Bard College graduate filed a formal complaint with the U.S. Department of Education this week, saying she wasn't permitted to discuss her alleged rape with a school official until she signed an agreement preventing her from discussing the assault" elsewhere.

In 2013, ten of the thirty-seven students and alumni who filed a lawsuit against Occidental College received cash payments but were barred from participating in the campus group, the Occidental Sexual Assault Coalition, that organized the campaign that resulted in the federal investigation. They were paid to be silent. Criminology professor Danielle Dirks told the *Los Angeles Times* that requiring "the women to remain silent and not to participate in campus activism could have a chilling effect at Occidental. Part of the reason so many women have come forward is because other assault survivors have been able to speak openly about their treatment."

What does it mean when what's supposed to be victory includes the imposition of silence? Or should we call it reimposition?

There are other ways victims are silenced: by being ridiculed, threatened, discredited, ostracized.

Rebecca Donner recently broke her own silence with an essay in the online magazine *Guernica* about being raped by her uncle when she was a teen, about how she was unable to speak and just nodded to her mother's questions, about how her family both blamed her for what happened and refused to believe it had happened, the familiar cognitive dissonance of victim-blaming. "I was told to get over what happened. I was told to remain silent. And until now, I've kept my mouth shut like a good girl." There are a million stories like this with their own sad details but the same pattern of denial and silencing.

Shame is a great silencer.

Silence is a burden that belongs or belonged to most of us, though some are more loaded with it than others, and some have become experts and geniuses in how to shove it aside, drop it, disown it. Elizabeth Smart, who at fourteen was kidnapped from her Salt Lake City home and raped for a period of months, said that the abstinence-only sex education she was given taught her that she was worthless and contaminated if she had sex before marriage. "And that's how easy it is to feel you no longer have worth. Your life no longer has value." That sense of worthlessness helped keep her captive, hopeless, with a sense that she had no good life to go back to. The campus antirape movement arose, in part, out of young survivors' refusal to be shamed into silence, and then to refuse shame altogether as at least a stance if not a psychic state.

So is politeness.

What we call politeness often means training that other people's comfort matters more. You should not disturb it, and you are in the wrong to do so, whatever is happening. I heard a short story read on the radio decades ago that stayed with me, a first-person narrative of a woman being groped on the New York subway, who was trying to figure out how to remove herself without implying the groper was in the wrong or offending him. It was a wry incident about how deeply ingrained are the instructions on being polite, comforting, pleasant, and unthreatening and how they can interfere with survival. I remember an incident in my early twenties where I was being menaced by a terrifying man on the street in the middle of the night, and I think of how it did not occur to me to flag down cars, make a ruckus, all the things that I would do when I was older and more confident about my assessments and my rights and less afraid to make a scene. Politeness, self-doubt, internal silencing can make younger women better targets. The philosopher Martha Nussbaum began graduate school at Harvard in 1969; she recalled recently that when her advisor "reached over to touch her breasts . . . she gently pushed him away, careful not to embarrass him."

Silence is also a legal status of powerlessness.
In 2015, Justice Ruth Bader Ginsburg brought up a 1982 Supreme Court case while hearing the case for same-sex marriage rights. "Marriage today is not what it was under the common law tradition, under the civil law tradition," said Ginsburg when Justices Roberts and Kennedy began to fret about whether the court had a right to challenge centuries of tradition. "Marriage was a relationship of a dominant male to a subordinate female," she explained. "That ended as a result of this court's decision in 1982 when Louisiana's Head and Master Rule was struck down."

Ginsburg, the second woman ever to serve on the Supreme Court, was referencing Louisiana's "head and master" law, which gave a husband unfettered right to dispose of jointly owned property without his wife's knowledge or consent. The test case involved a husband who mortgaged the house his wife had purchased with her earnings, to defend himself against charges of molesting their daughter. She had no voice in the disposal of her home, her earnings, the course of her life; what should have been hers or theirs was his alone.

Individuals and societies serve power and the powerful by refusing to speak and bear witness.
When witnesses refuse to speak up, they consent to another's loss of rights, agency, bodily integrity, or life. Silence protects violence.

Whole societies can be silent—and as with the Armenian genocide in Turkey, speaking about crimes can be made dangerous or illegal. The writer Orhan Pamuk was charged with "insulting Turkish identity" and forced to flee the country for speaking of a crime written out of textbooks and the official record.

There are specific ways in which specific people are silenced, but there is also a culture that withers away the space in which women speak and makes it clear men's voices count for more than women's. There are expert witnesses to the phenomenon.

In classical literature, Tiresias was a priest who was transformed into a woman as punishment, lived as one for seven years, and was then transformed back into a man. The gods went to him for firsthand testimony about gender and sexuality. In this era, trans people are expert witnesses to the way gender roles are enforced and reinforced. One whose testimony made a major impact more than a decade ago is Ben Barres, formerly Barbara Barres, a biologist at Stanford University. In 2006, he wrote in the journal *Nature* about the bias he had experienced as a woman in the sciences, from losing fellowships to less qualified male candidates to being told a boyfriend must have helped her with her math. He was told that he was smarter than his sister by a man who confused his former, female self for that sister. Some things he didn't notice until they stopped.

Then, like a good scientist, he observed carefully: "Anecdotes, however, are not data, which is why gender-blinding studies are so important. These studies reveal that in many selection processes, the bar is unconsciously raised so high for women and minority candidates that few emerge as winners." He spoke up to counter Harvard president Larry Summers's 2005 assertion that innate biological differences in aptitude explained why men did better than women in mathematics and the sciences. (At the time, the

Guardian noted, "During Dr Summers's presidency, the number of tenured jobs offered to women has fallen from 36% to 13%. Last year, only four of 32 tenured job openings were offered to women.") In a sidebar about his personal experience, Barres said wryly, "By far, the main difference I have noticed is that people who don't know I am transgendered treat me with much more respect: I can even finish a sentence without being interrupted by a man."

Men and women are given different kinds and amounts of space to occupy, literally, geographically, conceptually, and conversationally. This is measurable in movies, but exists in real life as well.

In 2010, the Geena Davis Institute on Gender in Media reported statistics from three years of Hollywood family films: "Of all speaking characters, 32.4% are female in G-rated films, 30% are female in PG-rated films and 27.7% are female in PG-13-rated films. Of 1,565 content creators, only 7% of directors, 13% of writers, and 20% of producers are female." In 2014, the institute conducted another study of films from the ten largest movie markets worldwide and found that more than two-thirds of speaking and named characters were male, and less than a quarter of films "depicted a girl or woman in the lead or sharing the story's journey with another main character."

A similar study of the 700 most successful movies from 2007–2014 by the Annenberg School for Communications found "In 2014's 100 most popular movies, 21 featured a female lead, about the same percentage as the 20 found among the top films of 2007. Of the top 100 films in 2014, two were directed by women. In 2007 there were three. Of the 700 films examined, three were directed by African Americans." None of the top 100 films of 2014 starred a woman over forty-five. A 2016 study of 2,000 films by *Polygraph* found that men had 88 percent of the leads.

When women are on the screen, they don't necessarily speak, and even when they speak they don't necessarily speak to each other, or they speak to each other about the men who remain central to the film. Graphic novelist Alison Bechdel came up with what's now well known as the Bechdel Test, the requirement that a movie have two female characters who talk to each other about something other than a man. It's a ridiculously low standard many films fail to meet. In the original *Star Wars* trilogy, women other than Princess Leia speak for 63 seconds of the films' 386 minutes, a recent investigation concluded. Those 63 seconds are divided among three women in the three films for what amounts to about a third of 1 percent of the running time.

But such films are not described as boys' or men's films, but as films for all of us, while films with a similarly unequal amount of time allocated to female characters would inevitably be regarded as girls' or women's films. Men are not expected to engage in the empathic extension of identifying with a different gender, just as white people are not asked, the way people of color are, to identify with other races. Being dominant means seeing yourself and not seeing others; privilege often limits or obstructs imagination.

The space to speak and the public sphere are intertwined, and this goes back millennia.

Classics scholar Mary Beard has analyzed the geographies of gender over the millennia. In a landmark essay from 2014, "The Public Voice of Women," she notes that silencing women begins almost as soon as Western literature does, in the *Odyssey*, with Telemachus telling his mother, Penelope, to shut up. Penelope is already chastely stranded at home and besieged by suitors while her husband leisurely wanders around the Mediterranean getting laid. (You can imagine a feminist revision in which Penelope enjoys her autonomy, takes some of the suitors as lovers, and maybe doesn't yearn for her husband's return; Margaret Atwood tried out a version of this with her *Penelopiad*.) Beard describes how having a voice—preferably a deep one—was considered definitive of masculinity, and the public sphere is the masculine sphere: "A woman speaking in public was, in most circumstances, by definition not a woman."

She became a much-attacked public figure herself in the twenty-first century, with the rise of social media:

> It doesn't much matter what line you take as a woman, if you venture into traditional male territory, the abuse comes anyway. It's not what you say that prompts it, it's the fact you're saying it. And that matches the detail of the threats themselves. They include a fairly predictable menu of rape, bombing, murder and so forth. But a significant subsection is directed at silencing the woman—"Shut up you bitch" is a fairly common refrain. Or it promises to remove the capacity of the woman to speak. "I'm going to cut off your head and rape it" was one tweet I got.

Which probably distinguishes her from most of the male classics professors at Cambridge. She told the *New York Times* in April 2016, "We have never escaped a certain male cultural desire for women's silence."

Women are often disqualified from participation in the kind of public life Beard speaks of.

There are myriad ways to remove women from public and professional life. Women who work in engineering speak of the ways in which their access to training and meaningful roles was denied; women who competed in chess speak of sexual harassment and denigration; the same stories emerge from women in many other fields. Women in politics are criticized for their appearances, for their voices, for being ambitious, for not serving their families full-time (or for not having families). Words like *strident* and *bossy* are largely reserved for women, the way that words like *uppity* are reserved for African Americans. Women in politics must not be too feminine, since femininity is not associated with leadership, but they must not be too masculine, since masculinity is not their prerogative; the double bind requires them to occupy a space that does not exist, to be something impossible in order not to be something wrong. Being a woman is a perpetual state of wrongness, as far as I can determine. Or, rather, it is under patriarchy.

I have looked at the reception of Rachel Carson's landmark 1962 book about the devastating effect of pesticides, *Silent Spring,* many times, appalled at the ways she was dismissed as hysterical, emotional, unqualified. As I was writing this book and researching another project, I read an oral history in which a man who had been on the board of the Sierra Club at the time *Silent Spring* was published, making Carson perhaps the best-known environmentalist of the 1960s, said: "I can't think of her name now but some woman who is not a scientist wrote a story about terrible pesticides." The only description he wanted to associate with this scientist—who held a master's and only for financial reasons failed to complete a PhD in zoology and genetics at Johns Hopkins, who had worked as a scientist for the federal government and then for Woods Hole Oceanographic Institution—was that she was "not a scientist."

That was an old man talking about a bygone era, but the idea that women are not qualified regardless of their qualifications is rampant now, as it was in Carson's time. Investigative journalist Suki Kim went undercover to report on conditions in North Korea, but her publishers insisted on casting her 2014 exposé as a memoir. A book about public and collective life was reframed as a personal journey for marketing reasons, but also with a sense that women belonged in the personal realm and, by extension, did not belong outside it. In 2016, she wrote in the *New Republic*,

> By casting my book as personal rather than professional—by marketing me as a woman on a journey of self-discovery, rather than a reporter on a groundbreaking assignment—I was effectively being stripped of my expertise on the subject I knew best. It was a subtle shift, but one familiar to professional women from all walks of life. I was being moved from a position of authority—What do you know?—to the realm of emotion: How did you feel?

She was kicked out of thinking about and knowing others, confined to her own emotions, as though the only realm in which she was competent was that of herself.

The imprisonment echoed the old order in which women were confined to the home and to private life, and public life was men's business. Of course the corollary is the exclusion of men, often, still, from emotional and personal life. Both realms matter, but economic, political, and social power depend on one's standing in the public realm. The revolution is for free movement of everyone, everywhere. It is not finished; it is under way; it has changed all the maps; they will change more.

IV: THE FLOODED CITY

"I want to write a novel about silence.
The things people don't say."

—**Virginia Woolf**

A feminist literature investigates the nature of those silences, their causes, and their effects, peaking in the 1970s and early 1980s with a plethora of essays on silence. Mary Wollstonecraft and nineteenth-century feminists addressed exclusion and powerlessness, including the exclusion from education. Suffragists pointed out that to be without the vote was to be silenced politically, excluded from full citizenship, self-determination, and the public sphere. Charlotte Perkins Gilman spoke in 1911 of women "hedged in with restrictions of a thousand sorts . . . the enforced ignorance from which women are now so swiftly emerging." In the era when women had gained the vote—in 1920 in the United States, in 1918 in Britain—but lacked so much else, the investigation of silence continued.

Virginia Woolf sounded the alarm in two landmark essays. The more famous *A Room of One's Own* came out in 1929, based on a pair of talks in 1928, about the practical, financial, social, and psychological restrictions on women writing and, by implication, having a voice. But what kind of a voice could she have? Adrienne Rich wrote, half a century later,

> I was astonished at the tone of effort, of pains taken, of dogged tentativeness in the tone of that essay. And I recognized that tone. I had heard it often enough, in myself and in other women. It is the tone of a woman almost in touch with her anger, who is determined not to appear angry, who is willing herself to be calm, detached, and even charming in a roomful of men where things have been said which are attacks on her very integrity. Virginia Woolf is addressing an audience of women, but she is acutely conscious—as she always was—of being overheard by men.

Woolf's "Professions for Women," originally delivered as a speech to the National Society for Women in 1931, addresses the other kind of voice, not the convincing one Rich criticized (and women's tone of voice is so often criticized), but the comforting one. She describes the internalized instructions to women to be pleasant, gracious, flattering, that can silence a real voice and real thoughts: a real self. She indicates that there are ways to speak that are silence's white noise: the platitudes and reassurances, the polite-nesses and denials that lubricate a system that perpetuates silence. You speak for others, not for yourself. Woolf talked about the voice within women that tells them, "Be sympathetic; be tender; flatter; deceive; use all the arts and wiles of our sex. Never let anybody guess that you have a mind of your own." She called that voice the Angel in the House and boasted of murdering her, out of necessity, so that she might have a voice. So that she might break the silence.

Half a century later, in her book *Pornography and Silence*, Susan Griffin quoted Norman Mailer on Marilyn Monroe: "She is a mir-ror of the pleasure of those who stare at her." Meaning that Monroe appeared, and she spoke, but how she appeared, what she said, was not to express herself, to be herself, but to serve others. Griffin comments, "Yet knowing that her symbolic existence was a mask he refuses to look behind this mask. And yet, had another self not ex-isted, a self to be lost and a self to be violated, the life of this actress would not have been a tragedy." It was an analysis of how someone can be visible, audible, yet silenced.

Monroe can stand in for any woman, all women who silence, hide, disguise, or dismiss aspects of themselves and their self-expression in pursuing male pleasure, approval, comfort, rein-forcement. This is not only erotic business; it's how a woman in the workplace or the classroom or on the street may have learned to navigate around male expectations, knowing if she is too confi-dent, commanding, or self-contained she may be punished. It has its analogies—my friend Garnette Cadogan has written eloquent-ly, excruciatingly, about how he as a Black man in public has to in-cessantly perform "not-a-criminal, not-a-threat" to assuage white fear and preserve himself. To be Black and a woman is to do double duty in this business of serving others.

Mailer, in calling Monroe a mirror of pleasure, fails to question what happens when the pleasure is routinely someone else's. It's a death of pleasure disguised as pleasure, a death of self in the service of others. It's silence wrapped in pleasing nothings. The portrait of Monroe, who died young in 1962, is a sort of book-end to bell hooks's observation about men's "psychic self-mutilation"—it is a portrait of the other kind of self-mutilation, to make a self to meet and serve those mutilated selves. A silence to meet the silence, silences that fit each other like a mold and casting, a ghost story.

Tillie Olsen gave a talk in 1962, published in 1965 in *Harper's*, that became part of her bestselling 1978 book *Silences*. Silence, or the desire to interrogate and annihilate it, had come of age. It begins, "Literary history and the present are dark with silences: some the silences for years by our acknowledged great; some silences hidden; some the ceasing to publish after one work appears; some the never coming to book form at all." In other words there were kinds of silence, one kind for what was said and what remained unsaid and another for who said it and who was permitted to speak.

She takes time to come to her real subject, as though she must establish her credentials first, her knowledge and care for the great literature by men. Then she turns to the silence of women in literature, noting that most who had literary careers had no children, because time to oneself and for oneself and one's voice is crucial to creation. That was about practical silence—the lack of time to build the palace of words that is an extended piece of writing—but there are many kinds of silence that pertained to women's experience at the time. The second half of the book is a broad collection of "asides, amulets, exhumations, sources," broadening the evidence for the silencing of women, and its consequences not only to women but to literature. A brief for the defense.

Betty Friedan's 1963 *The Feminine Mystique* was about "the problem that has no name," about American women who lived in material comfort yet in social and political annihilation in their exclusion from public life and power at home and in the world. It can be and has been critiqued as a book about middle-class white women; it can also be appreciated as a book that, during the war on poverty and the civil rights movement, said that gender was also a problem worth contemplating, and that naming is a crucial part of transformation.

In her 2010 book *At the Dark End of the Street*, Danielle L. McGuire argues that the Civil Rights Movement was itself silenced, in a way, when it was rewritten as a history of what a movement led by men (and forgotten women) did about everyone's rights. She restarts the history with Rosa Parks as an investigator of rape cases for the NAACP, thereby recasting the whole movement as launched by Black women for Black women's rights, an intersection ordinarily erased from the history of that boulevard.

In contrast, in 1969 Susan Sontag published an essay, "The Aesthetics of Silence," that is silent about gender. It's about male artists and uses the male pronoun to describe "the artist." She wrote about artists choosing silence, artists such as Marcel Duchamp and Arthur Rimbaud, for whom silence was a gesture of scorn or transcendence, a departure—but then she notes, "An exemplary decision of this sort can be made only after the artist has demonstrated that he possesses genius and exercised that genius authoritatively." It's the quiet some choose after being heard and valued—the antithesis of being silenced.

What gets called *second-wave feminism* is full of accounts of revelations about oppressions that were not previously named or described, and of the joy in recognizing even oppression: diagnosis is the first step toward cure and recovery. To speak of, to find definitions for what afflicted them brought women out of isolation and into power. The writings of the 1960s and 1970s are a literature of exploration, even revelation: people stumble forward, not sure what they are encountering, describing it awkwardly, reaching for new language for things that have not been described before, seeing the new undermine assumptions about the familiar, becoming people who belong to this new territory as much or more than to the old one, crossing over to a world being invented as they go.

Voyages of discovery: a key part of the feminist movement of the 1970s was "consciousness-raising groups," in which women talked to each other about their experience. Susan Griffin, an important participant in that era's feminism, told me that first they complained about housework, and then they started talking about rape and violence and the grim stuff, breaking through the shame that had kept them silent and alone. The poet Muriel Rukeyser's lines, "What would happen if one woman told the truth about her life? The world would split open," were often cited. What happened when many women told the truth about their lives? Silence itself became a key topic.

In 1977, Audre Lorde addressed the Modern Language Association with her landmark talk and essay considering race, gender, and orientation together, "The Transformation of Silence Into Language and Action" (published in 1984). It's a brief, dense, aphoristic essay with some of the urgency of a manifesto:

> My silences had not protected me. Your silence will not protect you. But for every real word spoken, for every attempt I had ever made to speak those truths for which I am still seeking, I had made contact with other women while we examined the words to fit a world in which we all believed, bridging our differences. And it was the concern and caring of all those women which gave me strength.

Lorde addressed the way that breaking silence was not only an act of courage but also of creation: "What are the words you do not yet have? What do you need to say? . . . Each of us is here now because in one way or another we share a commitment to language and to the power of language, and to the reclaiming of that language which has been made to work against us."

In 1978, Jamaican-born Michelle Cliff published "Notes on Speechlessness," which dealt with both avoidance and exploration of difficult truths. "Both withdrawal and humor are types of speechlessness. The obscuring and trivialization of what is real is also speechlessness." She wrote about bad dreams, wrote in fragments, wrote about herself but also about political and literary history, outed herself as a lesbian and addressed the way that passing as straight was a masquerade, another route around truth. Cliff's essay concludes that she will seek to eliminate what has eliminated her: "This means nothing more or less than seeking my own language. This may be what women will do."

Her lover and partner, Adrienne Rich, titled one of her books of poetry *The Dream of a Common Language*. The crucial poem in that book is "Cartographies of Silence": it opens, "A conversation begins/with a lie" and speaks of "the scream of an illegitimate voice." At the end of the long piece, truth breaks out like a new-growing thing, green. Many of the women who spoke up about silence were lesbians, including Griffin and Rich; some were also Black, including Cliff and Lorde. Though *intersectionality* is a term that has only recently come into wide use, these women understood what it means to operate at an intersection or at many. Rich's book came out the year before Cliff's essay; it includes, for the first time in her abundant body of work, lesbian love poems.

Two years later, in 1979, Rich published the essay anthology *On Lies, Secrets, and Silence*, in which her critique of Woolf's *A*

Room of One's Own, quoted above, appears. Elsewhere in the book she wrote,

> I believe any woman for whom the feminist breaking of silence has been a transforming force can also look back to a time when the faint, improbable outlines of unaskable questions, curling in her brain cells, triggered a shock of recognition at certain lines, phrases, images, in the work of this or that woman, long dead, whose life and experience she could only dimly try to imagine.

Once unaskable, the questions were being asked. In 1980, Rich added to her critique with the landmark essay "Compulsory Heterosexuality and Lesbian Existence," looking at the way that the identity and activity of a significant sector of women were over-looked or excluded and how that distorted the possibilities of living and understanding for all of us. She wrote of one popular feminist book of the time that it "ignores, specifically, the history of women who as witches, *femmes seules,* marriage resisters, spinsters, auton-omous widows, and/or lesbians—have managed on varying levels not to collaborate. It is this history, precisely, from which feminists have so much to learn and on which there is overall such blanketing silence." She was a great explorer.

She questioned heterosexuality as a norm: "The assumption that "most women are innately heterosexual" stands as a theoretical and political stumbling block for many women . . . the failure to examine heterosexuality as an institution is like failing to admit that the economic system called capitalism or the caste system of racism is maintained by a variety of forces." She writes of how les-bian lives had themselves been silenced, along with the possibility that heterosexuality is not natural "but something that has had to be imposed, managed, organized, propagandized and maintained by force." A new city of ideas and possibilities was being built, like a material city, by an accretion of projects, labors, decisions, and desires, and women were taking up residence in it.

The feminism of the 1970s is full of the joy and fury of recognition and the power that comes with recognition even of terrible things. What can be recognized can be remedied or resisted. In the third novel of her Naples quartet, Elena Ferrante describes her protagonist's discovery of feminist analysis in the 1970s: "How it is possible, I wondered, that a woman knows how to think like that? I worked so hard on books, but I endured them, I never actually used them, I never turned them against themselves." She sees, for the first time, what the world might look like from outside the assumptions that circumscribed her sense of possibility for herself, for her gender, for her language.

Some of the feminists of that era, notably Catherine MacKinnon and Andrea Dworkin, spoke out against one form of speech and representation—pornography—on the grounds that it contributed to the subjugation of women. Their work led to marches, demonstrations, legal cases, and bans that were overturned on free-speech grounds. Others in the movement defended pornography, either in and of itself or as free speech. (The defiant title of the journal *Off Our Backs* was mocked by the lesbian erotic magazine *On Our Backs*.) The antiporn feminists were much vilified, and they were also misremembered as a monolith with puritanical arguments, the foil to a liberatory libertinage.

It was more complicated than that (and the position that misogynistic pornography can encourage and model actual misogyny only requires you to accept the reasonable idea that representations have power and influence). As with Internet harassment in the present, the question was raised as to what is free speech, when some speech is designed to crush others' right and ability to speak and be heard.

Susan Griffin's 1981 book *Pornography and Silence* made an original argument: that mainstream pornography could be imagined not as liberatory speech, as free voices that should be heard, but as a particular kind of repression. She wrote that "pornography is an expression not of human erotic feeling and desire, and not of a love of the life of the body, but of a fear of bodily knowledge and a desire to silence eros." Pornography, in her view, was not erotic—if erotic meant the full and open experience of the body, the self, the emotions, and the other—but its opposite, full of "the metaphysics of Christianity . . . a modern building built on the site of the old cathedrals, sharing the same foundation."

That foundation includes loathing for the flesh, fury at desire, and a projection of that desire and that fury onto women. "We will come to see that 'the woman' in pornography, like 'the Jew' in anti-Semitism and 'the black' in racism is simply a lost part of the soul, that region of being the pornographic or the racist mind would forget and deny." Griffin's work since then has often sought the opposite: to remember, to admit, to enlarge the spaces in which we might be, dream, think, love, and celebrate the erotic and sensual.

The debate over pornography never stopped. In 1993, philosopher Rae Langton took up the topic in a remarkable, rigorous essay, "Speech Acts and Unspeakable Acts." Her exploration and analysis shed light far beyond pornography. She begins by refocusing the debate from what the content of speech is to what it does, what its power is. She points out that with language we marry, vote, render verdicts, give orders—or don't, if we lack the power to do so. A master saying, "I want food" to a slave is giving an order, the slave uttering the same words is making an appeal; the power each holds has everything to do with what their words mean and do. Or cannot do.

Langton makes the case that pornography carries authority as instruction as well as entertainment. She cites evidence to suggest that a high percentage of boys and young men regard men's satisfaction as a right and women's rights as an irrelevancy, as well as statistics on date rape and men who find women in pain erotic, and ties these things to porn culture. She outlines three kinds of silence. The first is the literal silence of intimidation or defeat. The second is when the speaker lacks a listener, a response. Then she concludes, "If pornography silences women, then it prevents women from doing things with their words."

This third kind of silence "happens when one speaks, one utters words, and fails . . . to perform the very act one intends." That act is of forbidding, of saying no. "It is indeed possible to silence someone . . . by making their speech acts unspeakable. . . . Consider the utterance 'no.' We all know how to do things with this word. However, in sexual contexts something odd happens. Sometimes a woman tries to use the 'no' locution to refuse sex, and it does not work. Refusal—in that context—has become unspeakable for her. In this case refusal is not simply frustrated but disabled." She explores the ramifications. "Someone learning the rules of the game from this kind of pornography might not even recognize an attempted refusal."

In her 2016 book *Girls and Sex,* Peggy Orenstein confirmed this erasure of voice, writing, "In a study of behaviors in popular porn, nearly 90% of 304 random scenes contained physical aggression toward women, who nearly always responded neutrally or with pleasure. More insidiously, women would sometimes beg their partners to stop, then acquiesce and begin to enjoy the activity, regardless of how painful or debasing." Elsewhere she notes, "Male and female college students who report recent porn use have been repeatedly found to be more likely than others to believe 'rape myths'; that only strangers commit sexual assault or that the victim 'asked for it.' . . . Female porn users are less likely than others to intervene when seeing another woman being threatened or assaulted and are slower to recognize when they're in danger themselves." That is, pornography has become instructional to women as well as men, and the instructions can deafen them to the voices of women, even to their own voices. Silence travels through many avenues.

I sometimes imagine porn as a compensatory parallel universe where male privilege has been augmented and revenge on female power is incessantly exacted. (Several years ago, Sam Benjamin wrote of his career as a young director in the capital of mainstream porn, the San Fernando Valley, "While my overt task at hand was to make sure that the girls got naked, my true responsibility as director was to make sure the girls got punished.") The immeasurably vast quantity of porn now in existence takes innumerable forms, and there are undoubtedly many exceptions. The mainstream product, however, seems more about the eroticization of power than the power of eros. Much in it that is described as heterosexual has a homoerotics of masculine triumph; it's like a sport in which the excitement is that women are endlessly defeated.

Silence and shame are contagious; so are courage and speech. Even now, when women begin to speak of their experience, others step forward to bolster the earlier speaker and to share their own experience. A brick is knocked loose, another one; a dam breaks, the waters rush forth. In the 1970s and 1980s, women talking about being molested as children and harassed and assaulted as adults had a huge practical impact. Laws and the enforcement of laws shifted. But these stories were also an assault on the impunity of authority, an authority that had often been indistinguishable from patriarchy. These stories said that authority was not necessarily to be trusted; that power was liable to be abused.

They were part of the great anti-authoritarian uprising that sometimes gets called *the sixties*, though *the sixties* are often reduced to young white men or to college students opposing a war, not acknowledging the breadth of many movements—civil rights and racial justice, including Native American and Latinx and Asian American as well as Black constituencies, gay and lesbian rights, disability rights, and environmental and anticolonial and anticapitalist critiques—that changed the foundations of our conversations. It was like wealth redistribution, but the redistribution was of audibility, credibility, value, participation, power, and rights. It was a great leveling, still going on—with backlashes seeking to shove people back into the silence from which they emerged.

Sometime in the teens of the twenty-first century, a new round of feminist conversation began, in part in response to atrocities and to the breaking of silence about atrocities, including campus rape (thanks to campus organizers, many of them rape survivors themselves). A number of stories garnered attention on an almost unprecedented scale, and the intersection of a less misogynistic mainstream media and feminists on social and alternative media generated a fiercely lively new conversation.

On a number of occasions in recent years, a notable case of gender violence—the Isla Vista massacre in Santa Barbara, Ghomeshi's attacks in Canada, football player Ray Rice's domestic violence in New Jersey, the Stanford rape case—has led women to testify on social media. Some just share the hashtags: #yesallwomen; #whyIstayed and #whyIleft, about domestic violence; #ibelieveher, in support of Ghomeshi's victims; #iwasrapedtoo, in response to the 2016 Stanford case; #notokay, the label for more than 27 million tweets from women telling their own stories about being sexually assaulted, in response to the videotape of presidential candidate Donald Trump talking about grabbing women "by the pussy."

Sometimes men participated in the sharing of the hashtags or supporting the speakers. As detailed elsewhere in this book, men actively speaking and acting on behalf of women's rights and feminism has been one of the steps forward in recent years (while there were also so many steps back). Social media also became the scene of furious campaigns to silence women who spoke up about violence against women and misogyny, and Twitter in particular tolerated extended campaigns of rape and death threats. It has become a new platform both for breaking the silence and trying to enforce it through threats and intimidation. "Online harassment has become the intellectual equivalent of street harassment," said media critic Jennifer Pozner after the Black actor Leslie Jones was harassed, insulted, and bullied into leaving Twitter. "It is the attempt to police and punish women for being in a public space. It's men and boys saying, 'Stay out of my playground.'"

Even the *Guardian* took stock of its vitriolic comments section in 2016 and reported that eight of its most attacked columnists were women, two were men of color, and the most attacked of all was feminist Jessica Valenti. This recent campaign to silence women online is far from over, though many things suggest that it is a backlash, an attempt to push back what has marched forward, to silence what has been heard.

There is always something unsaid and yet to be said, always someone struggling to find the words and the will to tell her story. Every day each of us invents the world and the self who meets that world, opens up or closes down space for others within that. Silence is forever being broken, and then like waves lapping over the footprints, the sandcastles and washed-up shells and seaweed, silence rises again.

We make ourselves in part out of our stories about ourselves and our world, separately and together. The great feminist experiment of remaking the world by remaking our ideas of gender and challenging who has the right to break the silence has been wildly successful and remains extremely incomplete. Undoing the social frameworks of millennia is not the work of a generation or a few decades but a process of creation and destruction that is epic in scope and often embattled in execution. It is work that involves the smallest everyday gestures and exchanges and the changing of laws, beliefs, politics, and culture at the national and international scale; often the latter arises from the cumulative impact of the former.

The task of calling things by their true names, of telling the truth to the best of our abilities, of knowing how we got here, of listening particularly to those who have been silenced in the past, of seeing how the myriad stories fit together and break apart, of using any privilege we may have been handed to undo privilege or expand its scope is each of our tasks. It's how we make the world.

An Insurrectionary Year

(2014)

I have been waiting all my life for what 2014 has brought. It was a year of feminist insurrection against male violence: a year of mounting refusal to be silent, refusal to let our lives and torments be erased or dismissed. It has not been a harmonious time, but harmony is often purchased by suppressing those with something to say. It was loud, discordant, and maybe transformative, because important things were said—not necessarily new, but said more emphatically, by more of us, and heard as never before.

It was a watershed year for women, and for feminism, as we refused to accept the pandemic of violence against women—the rape, the murder, the beatings, the harassment on the streets and the threats online. Women's voices achieved a power that seemed unprecedented, and the whole conversation changed. There were concrete advances—such as California's "Yes Means Yes" campus sexual consent law—but those changes were a comparatively small consequence of enormous change in the collective consciousness. The problems have not been merely legal—there have been, for example, laws against wife-beating since the nineteenth century, which were rarely enforced until the late 1970s and still can't halt the epidemic of domestic violence now. The fundamental problem is cultural. And the culture—many cultures, around the world—is beginning to change.

You can almost think of 2014 as a parody of those little calendars with the flower or the gemstone of the month. January was not for garnets; it was finally talking about online threats, and about Dylan Farrow's testimony that her adoptive father had molested her when she was seven. The conversation in April was about kidnapped Nigerian schoolgirls, and a Silicon Valley multimillionaire caught on video battering his girlfriend. May wasn't emeralds; it was the massacre of six people in Isla Vista, California, by a young misogynist and the birth of #yesallwomen, perhaps the most catalytic in a year of powerful protests online about women and violence.

September wasn't tourmaline; it was the release of a videotape that showed the American football player Ray Rice knocking out his fiancée in an elevator, and a renewed public conversation about domestic violence, accompanied by the hashtags #whyileft and #whyistayed. October brought, at last, a substantive conversation about street harassment, and an overwhelming response to the claims of fifteen women that Canada's most famous radio host, Jian Ghomeshi, had assaulted them.

Not all the allegations listed above have been proven true. But in some cases crimes that rarely received much coverage, if any—or had been treated as isolated incidents, or dismissed in various ways—were finally being recognized as part of a pattern of violence that constituted a genuine social crisis. Enough women were speaking up and being heard that the old troubles could no longer be dismissed. Thus it is that the circle of who has rights and who is heard widens, and though the two are not quite the same thing, they are inseparable.

In *Wanderlust*, my book on the history of walking, I described my own experience as a young woman:

> It was the most devastating discovery of my life that I had no real right to life, liberty and pursuit of happiness out of doors, that the world was full of strangers who seemed to hate me and wished to harm me for no reason other than my gender, that sex so readily became violence, and that hardly anyone else considered it a public issue rather than a private problem.

I was given advice about how to modify or limit my own life—rather than an affirmation that this was wrong and should change.

It was, and still is, a sort of blame-the-victim framework, this insistence that women modify their presence in public space, or just give up and stay in, rather than that we transform public space (or men) so that women have the right to walk down the street unharassed. The same blame has been applied to women in nearly every situation in which they are attacked by men, as a way of not blaming men. If I'm exhilarated this year that I've read more rape trial transcripts; victims' testimonies; accounts of murders, beatings, and threats; and rape tweets and misogynist comments than in probably all my other years put together, it's because violence against women is now a public issue. At last.

WAITING FOR THE WATERSHED

Why has this issue finally come to the fore? Why has something that's long been tolerated become intolerable—or rather, why are the people for whom it's intolerable finally part of the conversation? Why is it possible to talk about what has long been hushed up, glossed over, trivialized, and dismissed? I have been waiting for decades.

In June 1994, when Nicole Brown Simpson and Ronald Goldman were found murdered and her ex-husband's extensive history of battering and stalking her was revealed, I hoped we would have a real conversation about domestic violence and misogyny (which often results in collateral deaths of the target's friends, family members, coworkers, and others, and is a major factor in mass shootings in the United States). But O. J. Simpson hired a platoon of high-powered lawyers, who made him out to be the victim. Then the racism, corruption, and incompetence of the Los Angeles police and legal system let him off despite a monumental amount of evidence against him. (He was later found responsible for the murders in a civil trial.)

Throughout the televised trial, which dragged on for almost a year, there was little public discussion of domestic violence. As one advocate said, following the trial:

> There were some juror comments after the verdict that said, "Why were they talking about domestic violence when this is a murder trial?" When I realized the jurors didn't understand the connection between domestic violence and homicide and didn't know why domestic violence was being described to them, I realized that we were not doing a good enough job to get people to understand that this is a pretty common outcome.

Globally, 38 percent of all women murdered are killed by their intimate partners, according to a recent World Health Organization study.

Four years later, in 1998, the murder of Matthew Shepard in Laramie, Wyoming, brought worldwide attention to homophobia (though whether Shepard's sexual orientation was a motive in his murder has more recently been questioned). A year before Shepard's murder, a fifteen-year-old named Daphne Sulk was found dead outside Laramie—nude, bludgeoned, and stabbed seventeen times. A thirty-eight-year-old man who had been her lover (or her molester; she was below the age of consent) was convicted of voluntary manslaughter—not murder—shortly before Shepard's death. There was no national outrage over Sulk's murder, nor over the rape and murder of an eight-year-old Laramie girl, Christin Lamb, that summer.

All three of these deaths were monstrous, but two were barely news: business as usual, like many thousands of other violent crimes against women. If these crimes were addressed at all beyond the inner pages of a newspaper, they were treated as isolated incidents—the crimes of aberrant individuals. There had been titillating coverage of murders of white girls and women, but never the kind of indignation seen this year—the public assertion that this is part of a pattern, and the pattern has to change.

It's always something of a mystery why one particular incident becomes the last straw: why the suicide of Mohammed Bouazizi in Tunisia, in late 2010, set off the Arab Spring, rather than another event; why the killing of Michael Brown in Ferguson, Missouri, set off months of protests across the United States in a way that previous police killings of young Black men did not. It's the breaking loose of cumulative tension, the exhaustion of patience, the work of rage at what has been and the hope that there can be, must be, something better. I live in earthquake country, and here we know that the sudden shake-up is preceded by years or decades or centuries of tension. But that doesn't mean we know when an earthquake will come.

For violence against women, the long silence was ruptured late in 2012 with three stories: the sexual assault by a group of high school boys of an unconscious minor in Steubenville, Ohio; the unprecedented public account by Angie Epifano, a student at Amherst College in Massachusetts, of being raped and essentially punished for reporting it, while her assailant went free; and the attack on a young woman on a New Delhi bus, a rape so violent that the victim died of her injuries. Why did the earthquake come when it did? I can see several reasons.

The world in which these incidents happened had already changed. Thanks to the groundbreaking work of earlier generations, feminist voices on crucial issues have become normal and more or less mainstream. They appear in major newspapers and magazines, not just women's media or small progressive sites. And that has created a bulwark often able to resist the mischaracterization, trivialization, and silence on issues of concern to women.

Another factor is the rise of social media. The Internet is a strange place, where trolls, misogynists, and haters run rampant, from 4chan to Reddit to revenge porn sites to the fake indignation and real hate of Gamergate. Twitter has become the world's most effective delivery system for rape and death threats aimed at silencing and intimidating outspoken women. But at its best, social media is what its users make of it, and from the Arab Spring to this feminist insurgency, activists have created a sort of Greek chorus to the dramas of our lives and world.

Sometimes at big political demonstrations—against the war in Iraq in early 2003, for example—the thousands of placards with handwritten statements, jokes, and facts, for all their brevity, constitute a cumulative critique that covers a lot of angles. Social media can do the same, building arguments comment by comment, challenging, testing, reinforcing, and circulating the longer arguments in blogs, essays, and reports. It's like a barn raising for ideas: innumerable people bring their experiences, insights, analysis, new terms, and frameworks. These then become part of the fabric of everyday life, and when that happens, the world has changed. Then, down the road, what was once a radical idea becomes so woven into everyday life that people imagine that it is self-evident and what everyone always knew. But it's not; it's the result of a struggle—of ideas and voices, not of violence.

The most transformative such moment I witnessed this year was after the Isla Vista mass shooting—you remember, the incident in which a young man poisoned by "pickup artist" misogyny and possessed of a sense that all and any women owed him whatever he wanted, and that he had the right to administer collective punishment to the gender, killed six and wounded fourteen before he took his own life. He had set out to massacre members of a sorority but ended up killing anyone in his path, including other men. Many in the mainstream media rushed to assert that this was an isolated incident due to mental illness, and both the strong individual voices and the great collective roar on social media pushed back, hard, to insist that it was part of a pattern of misogynist violence and mass shootings.

Feminism succeeded in framing the story. A young woman coined the hashtag #yesallwomen and was hounded into silence and invisibility for a while, but what she started was unstoppable. Women began telling their stories of harassment, threats, violence, and fear, reinforced by each others' voices. Change begins at the margins and moves to the center; social media has made the edges more powerful and the transit from margin to center more swift—or maybe even blurred the distinction, as mainstream media sometimes scurries to catch up to a vibrant public debate in social and alternative media.

The public conversation about violence against women had begun to change: all of a sudden, the world was talking about how common such violence is and what excuses are made for it, calling out the men who were more concerned with excusing themselves than addressing the violence. (Thus it was that their aggrieved refrain, "Not all men . . ." —as in "not all men are rapists"—mutated into #yesallwomen, as in "Yes, all women have to deal with rape in one way or another.")

Many men who took the time to listen to what women were saying—on social media and elsewhere—realized for the first time what women have long endured. And the presence of actively engaged men was another sign of what seems to have been new and transformative this year—which is key, because changing the world for women means changing what is acceptable and admirable among men, where misogynist behavior has long been, in some circles, something to boast about. Some men wrote publicly about their realization of what kinds of hostility and danger women face, and how shocked they were to finally face it themselves. For decades, feminism was supposed to be women's work, though women can no more mitigate sexism without engaging men than people of color can address racism without the participation of white people.

AFTER THE RULES CHANGE

There is no better sign of how changes in the conversation changed the rules in 2014 than the treatment, late in the year, of the allegations against Bill Cosby and the charges against the Canadian radio star Jian Ghomeshi. The two men seemed to think the old rules still applied yet found that the world had changed since they last checked. Watching them try to brush aside the many claims against them was like watching a windup toy that has reached the wall; their wheels spun but they weren't going anywhere.

Ghomeshi was fired by the Canadian Broadcasting Corporation (CBC) for workplace sexual harassment in October 2014. He filed a wrongful termination lawsuit, demanding 55 million Canadian dollars and hired a fancy public relations firm. Most loudly, he issued a preemptive strike against potential accusers with a long-winded, widely circulated Facebook post that claimed, "I've been fired from the CBC because of the risk of my private sex life being made public as a result of a campaign of false allegations pursued by a jilted ex-girlfriend and a freelance writer." He claimed that the writer and the ex-girlfriend were distorting his perfectly consensual sexual activities out of malice, and that he was being attacked for being a sexual minority, a person into sadomasochism. In other words, he was the victim. It backfired.

The very language raised red flags for some readers, because the framework of viciously vindictive women who just lie to get men into trouble is maybe the tiredest stereotype around. It has been key to the routine discrediting of women who testify that they were assaulted. Ghomeshi's public gesture pushed the *Toronto Star* to publish a report based on testimony by four women about activities that were not consensual and not conventionally sexual (though they seemed to excite Ghomeshi). They claimed he had assaulted them, brutally and suddenly. The women withheld their names, because they knew they would be attacked, and their accounts were extensively attacked at first.

The consequences of going public with allegations are usually unpleasant. Needing to tell your story or wanting to see justice are motives that can override that reluctance. In the Ghomeshi case, more women came forward, five more immediately, then several more after that. Perhaps the most remarkable was respected actress and Royal Canadian Air Force captain Lucy DeCoutere, the first but far from the last to go on the record: "All of a sudden he choked me and slapped me in the face a few times," she said of a 2003 incident. "It was totally bewildering because I've never had anybody slap me in the face before. It's not a pleasant feeling to be choked and it came out of nowhere. It was unprovoked." By that time eight women had said they had been throttled and struck, and that the violence was not consensual sex play. By the accounts of these women, Ghomeshi was a man who desired to strangle and club women against their will, and often did.*

---

* In March 2016 Ghomeshi was acquitted on four counts of sexual assault and one of choking. At the trial, Ghomeshi's lawyer bullied the victims and the judge accused them of lying or concealing evidence. Ghomeshi avoided a second sexual assault trial by signing a peace bond.

So many assailants believed they would get away with it forever, because their victims lacked voices and credibility, or because the perpetrators could obliterate those voices and that credibility or terrorize them into silence. That the rules have, sometimes, to some extent, changed clearly baffles some of the perpetrators.

The entitlement to be the one who is heard, believed, and respected has silenced so many women who may never be heard, in so many cases. Because, as these stories come to light, you have to remember how many more never will—in cases where the victims died silent, as they have over generations, or have not yet found an arena in which they dare to come to voice, or have spoken up and only been mocked, shamed, or attacked for so doing. DeCoutere remarked: "The past month has seen a major shift in the conversation about violence against women. It has been an overwhelming and painful time for many people, including myself, but also very inspiring. I hope that victims' voices continue to be heard and that this is the start of a change that is so desperately needed."

The allegations against Cosby had been hovering in the wings for years, and even decades. A 2005 civil trial had gathered fifteen women who charged that he had sexually assaulted them, but the plaintiff settled out of court, and the case received only modest coverage. Most of his alleged victims had remained silent. Barbara Bowman, who reports being drugged and raped by Cosby in 1985, when she was seventeen, tells a typical story:

> A girlfriend took me to a lawyer, but he accused me of making the story up. Their dismissive responses crushed any hope I had of getting help; I was convinced no one would listen to me. That feeling of futility is what ultimately kept me from going to the police. I told friends what had happened, and although they sympathized with me, they were just as helpless to do anything about it. I was a teenager from Denver acting in McDonald's commercials.

He was Bill Cosby: consummate American dad Cliff Huxtable
and the Jell-O spokesman. Eventually, I had to move on with my
life and my career.

Most of his alleged victims were young and vulnerable, with
a vulnerability compounded by the lack of voice and credibility
young women have always had.

This autumn, standup comic Hannibal Buress called out Cosby
on stage: "Yeah, but you rape women, Bill Cosby, so turn the crazy down a couple notches." Many complained that it took a man
accusing Cosby to trigger a response—but perhaps Buress represented something else, a man who listened to and believed women
and thought what happened to them was important. An extended discussion about why women don't report rapes; about how, as
Bowman was, they are discredited, shamed, blamed, put on trial,
retraumatized; and about how rarely rapists are convicted had laid
the groundwork for people to understand that it was very likely that
these women were telling the truth and that the world had given
them little reason to try to bear witness earlier.

It's not really about Cosby or Ghomeshi. As we argued after the
Isla Vista mass shooting, perpetrators of violence against women
aren't anomalies or exceptional. They're epidemic. At best these celebrity cases give us occasions to discuss the meaning of these kinds
of crimes, to investigate the larger social questions and shift the
framework a little. Women who are assaulted by celebrities matter.
So do the Native women in the United States and Canada who face
exceptionally high rates of sexual assault, rape, and murder; the
women raped on campus, raped in the military, in prison; the sex
workers who face extraordinary difficulties when they are victims of
sexual assault. So do the women who are raped by police, of which
there have been a great many accounts and a few criminal convictions recently. This year at least some of the people who think going

to the police is a tidy solution may have learned that the police can be incredulous, unresponsive, abusive, or ineffective. Only a small percentage of rapes are reported, and only a small percentage of those reported result in convictions.

What matters most in celebrity cases may not be that a few are belatedly held accountable for past crimes. It's the message that these cases deliver: that the age of impunity is over; that in the future, it will not be so easy to get away with committing such crimes. In other words, the world has changed enough to change the odds for victims and perpetrators. Women have voices now.

AFTER SHAME

This month, an arts administrator I know decided to speak up, forty-four years after the fact, about how she was, at nineteen, despondent, on a drug overdose in a seedy hotel, gang-raped by the men she had asked for help and then humiliated by a doctor who blamed her for what had happened. She recalls the doctor told her that "I was in no position to be pressing charges," and so came four decades of silence. This winter felt like the right time to break it.

Shame has been a huge factor in the silence of women—and men—who are victims of sexual assault. Shame has silenced people, isolated them, and let the crimes continue. The names of rape victims were traditionally not reported by the media to "protect" them, but this tradition had the additional effect of insisting that they had been shamed, keeping them invisible, isolated, and silent. "Who would want this 15 minutes of—not fame—shame?" asked one of Cosby's accusers, explaining why she hadn't spoken up before. Rape is an assault not only on the victim's body but also on their rights, their humanity, and their voice. The right to say no, to self-determination, is taken away; shame perpetuates this silencing. Shame, says a website for survivors, involves destruction of self-respect, the deliberate efforts by the attacker to make her do things against her will, to make her feel dirty, disgusting, and ashamed. Feelings of shame may also affect her decision to report the crime to the police or to reach out for help . . . She may also believe her previous sexual experiences and details of the assault will be scrutinized.

"'He said/she said' is always about discrediting 'she said,'" a campus professional who handles sexual assault cases told me the other day. It worked well until now. The tables have turned. When actress Jennifer Lawrence's nude photographs were stolen and distributed online, she started on the usual route of being ashamed and apologetic, but then revolted: "Anybody who looked at those pictures, you're perpetuating a sexual offense. You should cower with shame," she thundered. A couple of months later, a California man went to prison for a year for using nude photographs to harass and humiliate his ex-girlfriend in front of her employers and others; California is one of several states to have passed revenge porn laws since the category arose.

Emma Sulkowicz, an art student at Columbia University in New York, whose response to the lack of legal or institutional remedy after she accused a fellow student of raping her in her own dorm-room bed has been to carry a mattress every moment she's on campus, began with a more conventional reaction. Her first response was to stay quiet; her second, to ask the university to adjudicate the situation, but neither that nor going to the police offered her a response she considered meaningful. So she turned to art, and, as a fellow student said, she "cracked shame not only for herself but cracked shame in all of us." It must be very unpleasant to find out you've violated a brilliant artist whose public performance about you has drawn international attention and widespread support.

Shame kept people silent, often for decades or a lifetime, and isolated; speaking up has formed communities and sparked activism. It's hard to imagine Sulkowicz's defiant gesture without the extraordinary campus antirape movement, including campus rape survivors-become-activists such as Andrea Pino and Annie Clark and organizations such as Safer (Students Active for Ending Rape), that has challenged universities across the United States. Sulkowicz's genius was to make her burden tangible, and in so doing make it something others could share. Solidarity has been a big part of this feminist movement against violence.

In Sulkowicz's case, you could actually carry that mattress. In late September, I watched her coming out of a school building with a bearded blond student helping her until a group of young women swooped up to take charge of the mattress for a few hours. They hoisted the long blue mattress high, like pallbearers with a coffin, for a few hours one beautiful autumn morning at Columbia, giggling and chatting like young women anywhere, but also ferociously intent on solidarity in the form of transporting this symbol of conflict up stairs and along walkways. Sulkowicz made rape a visible burden, and though she will carry her mattress as long as both she and her alleged assailant are at Columbia University, she marks the return of shame to its rightful owners.

In one of the most conservative corners of the United States, Norman, Oklahoma, three high school students reported being raped by the same fellow student. The alleged rapist, like the high school boys who documented their sexual assault of a fellow student in Steubenville, Ohio, in 2012, and like so many others, circulated a video of the latest of these assaults in September 2014. In Norman, as with so many previous high school cases, the alleged victims were mocked and bullied by peers and unprotected by administrators, who encouraged them to withdraw from school. Up to that point, it was like too many cases before.

Then the tide changed: another male student, distressed by the alleged rapist's account of his actions, recorded what amounted to a confession as well as a boast, and in December 2014 the alleged rapist was charged by the police. A group of women, including a fellow high school student, Danielle Brown, took up the cause, launched the hashtag #yesalldaughters, and made demands on the school. On November 24, 2014, hundreds of students walked out in protest as part of a demonstration said to have numbered 1,500 people. Maybe we won't have to read the same story over and over; maybe young men won't think that such crimes enhance their status or that they have impunity. Maybe shame will be returned to its rightful owners.

The North American stories I'm telling here are about a shift in power that is partly a shift in whose story gets told and believed, and who does the telling.

This has not been a harmonious year, and male rage is definitely part of the landscape—the trolls, men's rights movement misogynists, Gamergate ranters, and the perpetrators of the actual violence, which has not stopped. The histrionic response to California's "Yes Means Yes" campus consent law shows that some heterosexual men are alarmed that they will now have to negotiate their erotic and social interactions with human beings who have voices and rights backed up by law. In other words, they are unhappy that the world has changed—but the most important thing is that it has. Women are coming out of a silence that lasted so long no one can name a beginning for it. This noisy year is not the end—but perhaps it is the beginning of the end.

Feminism:
The Men Arrive

(2014)

What do the prime minister of India, retired National Football League punter Chris Kluwe, and superstar comedian Aziz Ansari have in common? It's not that they've all walked into a bar, though Ansari could probably figure out the punch line to that joke. They've all spoken up for feminism this year, part of an unprecedented wave of men actively engaging with what's usually called "women's issues," though violence and discrimination against women are only women's issues because they're things done to women—mostly by men, so maybe they should always have been "men's issues."

The arrival of the guys signifies a sea change, part of an extraordinary year for feminism, in which the conversation has been transformed, as have some crucial laws, while new voices and constituencies joined in. There have always been men who agreed on the importance of those women's issues, and some who spoke up, but never in such numbers or with such effect. And we need them. So consider this a watershed year for feminism.

Take the speech the generally malevolent Indian prime minister

Narendra Modi gave on that country's Independence Day. Usually it's an occasion for boosterism and pride. Instead, he spoke powerfully of India's horrendous rape problem. "Brothers and sisters, when we hear about the incidents of rape, we hang our heads in shame," he said in Hindi. "I want to ask every parent [who has] a daughter of 10 or 12 years age, you are always on the alert, every now and then you keep on asking where are you going, when would you come back. . . . Parents ask their daughters hundreds of questions, but have any parents ever dared to ask their son as to where he is going, why he is going out, who his friends are? After all, a rapist is also somebody's son. He also has parents."

It was a remarkable thing to say, the result of a new discourse in that country in which many are now starting to blame perpetrators, not victims—to accept, as campus antirape activists in the United States put it, that "rapists cause rape." That act, in other words, is not caused by any of the everyday activities women have been blamed for when men assault them. This in itself represents a huge shift, especially when the analysis comes from the mouths of men. And from this violently conservative man, the words seemed remarkable—not because they were evidence of some emerging virtue in Modi, but because he seemed to be a conduit for arguments framed elsewhere: feminism was so powerful a force it emerged even from his mouth.

The Obama administration, too, recently launched a campaign to get bystanders, particularly men, to reach out to protect potential victims of sexual assault under the rubric "It's On Us." Easy as it might be to critique that slogan as a tone-deaf gesture, it's a landmark all the same, part of a larger response in this country to campus rape in particular.

And here's what it all means: the winds of change have reached our largest weathervanes. The highest powers in the country have begun calling on men to take responsibility not only for their own conduct but also for that of the men around them, to be agents of change.

WHEN X DOESN'T EQUAL Y

Feminism needs men. For one thing, the men who hate and despise women will be changed, if they change, by a culture in which doing horrible things to, or saying horrible things about, women will undermine rather than enhance a man's standing with other men.

There are infinite varieties of men, or at least about 3.5 billion different ones living on Earth now, Klansmen and human rights activists, drag queens and duck hunters. For the purposes of feminism, I'd like to delineate three big blurry categories. There are the allies, mentioned above (and below). There are the raging misogynists and haters in word and deed. You can see them in various places online, where they thrive (and seem to have remarkable amounts of time on their hands): the men's rights forums, for instance, where they endlessly stoke the flames of their resentment, and the guys on Twitter who barrage almost any outspoken woman with threats and insults. Take the threat not just to kill media analyst Anita Sarkeesian for daring to speak up about sexism in video games but to launch a massacre of women at a speech she was to give at the University of Utah. Sarkeesian's not the only one in that world to receive death threats. And don't forget all the gamers who have gone down the rabbit hole of misogynist conspiracy theories under the hashtag #Gamergate.

Their position was recently attacked in a striking rant by avid gamer, former pro football player, outspoken queer rights advocate, and feminist Chris Kluwe. He told his gaming brethren, in one of his more polite passages:

> Unfortunately, all you #Gamergaters keep defending this puerile filth, and so the only conclusion to draw is the logical one: That you support those misogynistic cretins in all their mouthbreathing

glory. That you support the harassment of women in the video game industry (and in general). That you support the idiotic stereotype of the "gamer" as a basement-dwelling sweatbeast that so many people have worked so hard to try and get rid of.

Someone then tweeted at Kluwe, "Go fuck yourself you stupid cunt. Gamergate is not hating on women." To which I'd like to append a variation on Lewis's Law ("all comments on feminism justify feminism"): the plethora of men attacking women and anyone who stands up for women in order to prove that women are not under attack and feminism has no basis in reality are apparently unaware that they're handily proving the opposite.

There are so many rape and death threats these days. In Sarkeesian's case, the University of Utah declined to take the threat of a massacre at the school seriously (despite the fact that weapons could legally be brought into the lecture hall), because she gets death threats all the time, and as a result, she had to cancel her own lecture.

So there are the allies and the haters. And then there are a slew of men who may mean well but enter the conversation about feminism with factually challenged assertions that someone—usually, in my experience, a woman—will spend a lot of time trying to rectify. They may be why Elizabeth Sims started a website called The Womansplainer: "For men who have better things to do than educate themselves about feminism."

Other times they try to refocus anything said about women's woes on men's woes. Reading men's comments online about campus rape, for example, you'd think that we face an epidemic of unconscious but malicious young women regularly impaling themselves on innocent bystanders for the purpose of getting them in trouble. *Forbes* recently ran, and then scrambled to delete, a tirade by a former president of an MIT fraternity titled, "Drunk Female Guests Are the Gravest Threat to Fraternities."

Sometimes, men insist "fairness" means admitting that men suffer from women just as women do from men, or even that they suffer more. You might as well argue that white people suffer from racism exactly as much as Black people, or that there are no hierarchies of privilege and degrees of oppression in this world. Some do.

It's true, for example, that women do commit domestic violence, but the consequences are drastically dissimilar in both numbers or severity. As I wrote in *Men Explain Things to Me*, domestic violence is

> the number one cause of injury to American women; of the two million injured annually, more than half a million of those injuries require medical attention while about 145,000 require overnight hospitalizations, according to the Centers for Disease Control and Prevention, and you don't want to know about the dentistry needed afterward. Spouses are also the leading cause of death for pregnant women in the United States.

Pregnant women are not, however, a leading cause of death for spouses of pregnant women. There's just no equivalency.

Not all men get this, but some do (and that might make a nice hashtag). I saw standup comic Aziz Ansari perform a routine focused on sexual harassment. "Creepy dudes are everywhere," he said, while describing a woman who had to take refuge in a pet store for an hour to shake off a guy following her. He pointed out that men never have to deal with women whipping out their genitals and masturbating at them in public or harassing them in other similarly grotesque ways. "Women just don't do that shit!" he exclaimed. (He credited his girlfriend with turning him into a feminist.)

The comedians Nato Green, W. Kamau Bell, Elon James White, and Louis C. K. are among the other feminist standup comics now speaking out, and Jon Stewart has had some fine feminist moments.

It's great that men are not only in the conversation but an increasingly witty part of it as well. Black men such as Bell, White, and Teju Cole have been exceptionally perceptive, articulate, and outspoken on the issues, perhaps because oppression understands oppression.

Cole wrote:

> Last night, reading the accounts by women who had been assaulted by Cosby, I was overcome with sorrow.
>
> Tricky to say anything about this, but silence is simply not an option. This is everybody's business. But I'll say some things to the men who are reading.
>
> We men benefit, all of us men benefit, from rape culture. We benefit from the pain it causes women because we sprint ahead obliviously; we benefit from the way it knocks them off circuit and opens space for us; we benefit from the way it dehumanizes them so that our own humanity can shine more greatly; and we benefit from the aura of power it gives us as perpetrators or as beneficiaries. And because we benefit, explicitly or implicitly, we are not vociferous enough in our opposition to it.
>
> We must be allies in this, in a subsidiary but vital role, to the generations of women who have been fighting it since forever. Why should it be easy? It can't be.

THE OBSESSION ABOUT FALSE RAPE ACCUSATIONS: A HANDY PULLOUT SECTION

Of course, the old ideas are out in force, too. Pretty much every time someone raises the subject of rape in my hearing (or online reading), a man pops up to raise the "issue" of "false rape accusations." Seriously, it's almost inevitably the first thing out of some guy's mouth; men appear obsessed with the subject, and it often becomes a convenient way of changing the focus from widespread female victims to exceedingly rare male victims. As a result, I've assembled this handy pullout guide to the subject in the hope that I never have to address it again.

Rape is so common in our culture it's fair to call it an epidemic. After all, what else could you call something that impacts nearly one in five women (and one in seventy-one men) directly and, as a threat, virtually all women, that is so pervasive it modifies how we live and think and move through the world for most of our lives? Actual instances in which women have untruthfully claimed a rape occurred simply to malign some guy are extremely uncommon. The most reliable studies suggest that about 2 percent of rape reports are false, which means that 98 percent are real. Even that statistic doesn't mean that 2 percent are false rape accusations, because saying you were raped if you weren't isn't the same thing as claiming a specific person raped you when he didn't. (No one sifts for the category of false rape accusation of an individual, by the way.) Still, those stats don't stop men from bringing the subject up again and again and again. And again.

Here's what such accusations sound like in translation:

Her: There's an epidemic afflicting my people!

Him: I'm worried about this incredibly rare disease I heard about (but didn't research) that could possibly afflict a member of my tribe!

Or maybe it sounds like this:

Her: Your tribe does horrible things to mine, which is well documented.

Him: Your tribe is full of malicious liars. I don't really have evidence of that, but my feelings are more rational than your facts.

Keep in mind, by the way, when you consider those figures on rape, that most rapes are not reported. Of the rapes that are, most are not prosecuted. Of those that are prosecuted, the great majority fail to achieve convictions. Bringing rape charges is generally not a fun and effective way to seek either revenge or justice, and falsely reporting a crime is itself a crime, something the police do not generally look kindly upon.

Hundreds of thousands of rape kits collected by the police in this country were, we now know, never sent to crime labs for testing, and a few years back, various cities—New Orleans, Baltimore, Philadelphia, and St. Louis—were exposed for not even bothering to file police reports on tens of thousands of rape claims. This should help convince you that the system does not work that well for rape victims. And remember who the police are: an increasingly militarized, mostly male group with high rates of domestic violence and some notable rape charges of their own recently. In other words, they're not always the most sympathetic people for women—particularly nonwhite women, sex workers, trans women, and other marginalized groups—to talk to about male sexual misconduct.

People also often wonder why colleges adjudicate rape cases themselves rather than report them to the police, particularly since many of them don't do it well. The reasons are numerous, including the fact that campuses are required under Title IX (a 1972 amendment to the 1964 federal Civil Rights Act) to ensure equal access to education for everyone. Sexual assault undermines that equality under the law. Then there's the fact that the criminal justice system is broken when it comes to sexual violence and that many rape survivors regard dealing with the legal system as a second round of violation and humiliation. Sometimes charges are dropped simply because the victim can't endure the process any longer. Appealing a guilty verdict on rape in the hope that the victim will be unable to endure another trial has become, I have been told, a tactic for overturning convictions.

And now, back to those false rape accusations. In *Men Explain Things to Me*, I added this footnote:

False accusations of rape are a reality, and a relatively rare one, though the stories of those convicted falsely are terrible. A British study by the Crown Prosecution Service released in 2013 noted that there were 5,651 prosecutions for rape in the period studied, versus only 35 prosecutions for false allegations of rape (or more than 160 rapes for every false allegation, well under 1 percent). And a 2000 U.S. Department of Justice report cited these estimates for the United States: 322,230 rapes annually, resulting in 55,424 reports to police, 26,271 arrests, and 7,007 convictions—or slightly more than 2 percent of rapes counted and 12 percent of rapes reported resulted in jail sentences.

In other words, reporting a rape is not likely to get someone jailed, and though perhaps 2 percent of rape charges are false, only slightly more than 2 percent of all charges result in convictions. (Some estimates go as high as 3 percent.) In other words, there are an awful lot of unpunished rapists out there. And most rapists, when accused or charged, do not admit to committing rape. Which means we have a host of rapists out there who are also liars, and maybe the lies that abound are by men who have raped, not by women who have not been raped.

Of course false-rape allegations have happened.* My friend Astra Taylor points out that the most dramatic examples in this

---

* Since I wrote this essay, *Rolling Stone* published and retracted a story on rape at the University of Virginia. The article focused on one alleged victim, whose statements were not fact-checked and were not accurate. The mainstream media and the Twittersphere become obsessed with the case and gave the victim and her falsehoods massive coverage, in such a way as to suggest that false rape charges were the major problem at UVA, a school under federal investigation and charged with mishandling dozens of incidents of sexual assault dating back many years. In 2004, the *Charlottesville Hook* had reported, "In the same span, 60 UVA students reported they'd been sexually assaulted, many by fellow students. Yet, according to various sources in the UVA administration, not one sexual offender has been expelled or even suspended from the school in the past five years." But after the *Rolling Stone* debacle, dozens of news stories gave the impression there was only one rape story at UVA and it was false.

country were when white men falsely accused Black men of assaulting white women. Which means that if you want to be indignant on the subject, you'll need to summon up a more complicated picture of how power, blame, and mendacity actually work. There have been incidents—the infamous Scottsboro Boys gang-rape case of the 1930s, for example—where white women were also pressured by the authorities to lie in order to incriminate Black men. In the Scottsboro case, one of the accusers, seventeen-year-old Ruby Bates, later recanted and told the truth, despite the threats against her.

Then there's the Central Park jogger case of 1989 in which the police coerced false confessions from, and the judicial system (including a woman prosecutor) convicted and jailed, five innocent African American and Latino teens. The white victim, who had been beaten nearly to death, had no memory of the incident and was not a witness against them. In 2002, the real assailant confessed and the five were exonerated, but only after their youths were spent in prison for crimes they didn't commit. Even in 2016 Donald Trump was proclaiming the guilt of these innocent men. Convicting the innocent tends to result from corruption and misconduct in the justice system, not just a lone accuser. Of course, there are exceptions. My point is that they are rare.

The false-rape-allegation obsession apparently arises from a number of things, including the delusion that they are common and the enduring slander that women are naturally duplicitous, manipulative, and unreliable. The constant mention of the issue suggests that there's a weird kind of male confidence that comes from a sense of having more credibility than women. And now that's changing. Maybe by confidence I mean entitlement. Maybe what these feminist guys are saying is: men are finally going to be held accountable and that frightens them. Maybe it's good for them to be frightened—or at least accountable.

WHAT MAKES A PLANET INHABITABLE

The situation as it has long existed needs to be described bluntly. Let's just say that a significant number of men hate women, whether the stranger harassed in the street, the Twitter user threatened into silence online, or the wife who's beaten. Some men believe they are entitled to humiliate, punish, silence, violate, and even annihilate women. As a consequence, women face a startling amount of everyday violence and an atmosphere of menace, as well as a host of smaller insults and aggressions meant to keep us down. It's not surprising, then, that the Southern Poverty Law Center classifies some men's rights groups as hate groups.

In this context, consider what we mean by rape culture. It's hate. Those sports-team and fraternity rapes are predicated on the idea that violating the rights, dignity, and body of another human being is a cool thing to do. Such group acts are based on a predatory-monster notion of what masculinity is, one to which many men don't subscribe but one that affects us all. It's also a problem that men are capable of rectifying in ways women are not.

The other evening, I left a talk on what makes a planet inhabitable—temperature, atmosphere, distance from a star—by an astrophysicist I know. I'd thought about asking a young man, a friend of a friend of mine, to accompany me to my car in the very dark park outside the California Academy of Sciences, but the astrophysicist and I fell to talking and walked to the car together without even questioning the necessity of it, and then I drove her to her car.

A couple of weeks earlier, I joined Emma Sulkowicz and a group of young women who were carrying a mattress between classes at Columbia University. As mentioned earlier, Sulkowicz is an art major who reported being raped and received nothing that resembled justice either from the campus authorities or the New York Police Department. In response, she is bearing witness to her plight with a performance-art piece that consists of carrying a dorm-room mattress with her whenever she's on campus, wherever she's going.

The media response has been tremendous.[†] A documentary film team was along that day, and the middle-aged camerawoman remarked to me that, if campus consent standards had existed when she was young, if the right of women to say no and the obligation of men to respect women's decisions had been recognized, her life would have been utterly different. I thought about it for a moment and realized: so would mine. So much of my energy between the ages of twelve and thirty was given over just to surviving predatory men. The revelation that humiliation, harm, and maybe even death was liable to be inflicted on me by complete strangers and casual acquaintances because of my gender and that I had to be on watch all the time to avoid such a fate—well, that's part of what made me a feminist.

I care passionately about the inhabitability of our planet from an environmental perspective, but until it's fully inhabitable by women who can walk freely down the street without the constant fear of trouble and danger, we will labor under practical and psychological burdens that impair our full powers. Which is why, as someone who thinks climate is the most important thing in the world right now, I'm still writing about feminism and women's rights. And celebrating the men who have made changing the world slightly more possible or are now part of the great changes under way.

---

† After I wrote that, Sulkowicz was subjected to massive attacks on social media, in the men's rights movement, and elsewhere. In 2016, a search on her name turns up "Emma Sulkowicz" as the first result, "Emma Sulkowicz liar" as the second result. Posters were put up around the Columbia campus calling her a "pretty little liar" and a Twitter account called @fakerape went after her until it was suspended.

One Year after
Seven Deaths

(2015)

In 1988 the photographer Richard Misrach found a couple of *Playboy* magazines that had been used for target practice near the Nevada Nuclear Test Site, where more than a thousand US and British nuclear weapons had been detonated. As he looked, a breeze ruffled the pages of the magazine to a picture of Ray Charles singing. Every page of the magazine had a starry constellation of bullet holes— jagged, with rips going into the paper beyond the hole—scattered across it. Misrach recalls that Ray Charles's "ecstasy was transformed into a scream by a bullet that had ripped through the magazine. I realized that the women on the covers of both magazines were the intended targets, but that the violence that was directed specifically at the women symbolically penetrated every layer of our society. Every aspect of our society . . . was riddled with violence."

I thought of his big color photographs of male and female celebrities, landscapes, products, movie scenes, all ripped through by bullets, and of his comment, when I began to contemplate, again, the Isla Vista massacre a year ago today. On the evening of May 23,

2014, a twenty-two-year-old went on a rampage that left six dead and injured many more, grazed by bullets or slammed into by his car, before he killed himself with his handgun.

The weather was balmy that night in Isla Vista, a coastal development next to the University of California–Santa Barbara, full of pizza and burrito shops with gimmicky names, fraternity and sorority houses, apartment buildings. Students were out skateboarding, bicycling, walking around with friends in shorts and T-shirts and swimsuits. The killer, whose name should not be remembered, who should not be glorified as the Columbine killers were, had no friends, though he had lived there for nearly three years. He had long planned a bloodbath as revenge on a world he thought owed him sex, adoration, friendship, success. His hatred was particularly directed at women and girls and the men who enjoyed their company.

The autobiography the young man, who grew up on the edge of the Hollywood movie industry, posted online that day is notable for its shallowness and its entitlement. Those are harsh words, but there's no other way to describe his utter lack of empathy, imagination, and engagement with the life of others. He's often described as mentally ill, but he seems instead to be someone who was exceptionally susceptible to the madness of the society around him, our society at its worst.

His misogyny was our culture's misogyny. His sad dream of becoming wealthy, admired, and sexually successful by winning the lottery was a banal, widely marketed dream. His preoccupation with brand-name products and status symbols was exactly what the advertising industry tries to inject into our minds. His fantasy of attaining power and status at the point of a gun is the fantasy sold to us by the gun lobby and the action movies in which some invulnerable superman unerringly shoots down the bad guys, a god made a god by his gun. "My first act of preparation was the purchase

[of] my first handgun," he wrote about his long-planned rampage. "After I picked up the handgun, I brought it back to my room and felt a new sense of power. I was now armed. *Who's the alpha male now, bitches?* I thought to myself, regarding all of the girls who've looked down on me in the past."

That day, as he had planned, he stabbed to death three young men in his apartment, apparently ambushing them one at a time. Two were his roommates, one a visitor: Weihan Wang, age twenty, Chen Hong, also twenty, and George Chen, nineteen. He then set out with his guns for the sorority he thought had the most beautiful women and banged on the door, hoping to go in and massacre them all—"full of hot, beautiful blonde girls; the kind of girls I've always desired but was never able to have because they all look down on me. They are all spoiled, heartless, wicked bitches." Alarmed by the angry, persistent pounding on the sorority's front door, no one opened it. The killer instead shot three women out front, twenty-two-year-old Katherine Cooper, nineteen-year-old Veronica Weiss, and a third woman who survived, aided by passersby and then sheriff's deputies. Back in his car, he swerved to hit passersby, hurling some with the impact, smashing others, missing others with his car, and spraying others with more bullets. He injured fourteen people, in addition to the six he killed.

The last person he murdered before he took his own life was Christopher Michaels-Martinez, who was out with his friends and the last one to enter the convenience store where they took shelter. On May 23, 2014, at about 9:30 p.m., a bullet, says the sheriff's report "entered the left side of the chest and exited the right side of the chest, puncturing the liver and right ventricle of the heart." Christopher Michaels-Martinez, an athletic twenty-year-old English major out with his friends, died immediately on the floor of the convenience store, despite the attempts of a nineteen-year-old woman to help him. She recalled a few days later, at the impromptu memorial of candles and flowers in the sidewalk outside the store, "I was giving him CPR, looked down, and recognized his face. He was the first person I met at freshman orientation."

"I would give the rest of my days for one more day with Christopher," Richard Martinez, Christopher's father, told me a couple of weeks ago. "But that's not gonna happen. So instead I do this"—this being his gun-control advocacy work with Everytown for Gun Safety. "I don't want any other parents to go through losing a child as beloved as our son was. I feel this is about saving lives." Six other people young people died that night too. All of them had families; all of them must have had grief akin to Richard Martinez's. And the young man's mother. And cousins, friends, a girlfriend, fellow students.

And his uncle, Alan Martinez, a San Francisco architect who's a friend of mine, who loved his nephew, recalls discussing Cicero, the Alhambra, AIDS, Buddhism, and everything else under the sun with the boy. There's a photograph of uncle and nephew lying on their backs on a green California hillside, both laughing at the same joke or just the joy of the moment. And then there was the press conference the day after, where Alan stood at Richard's side and Richard said, in a voice thick with anguish, "Not one more," which became the slogan for his campaign for gun control.

Richard Martinez, an imposing dark-haired man with a whitening beard, last spoke with Christopher a few hours before his death; the UCSB student was excited about his upcoming year studying abroad in London. Richard wonders if they had stayed on the phone a moment longer, or ended the conversation a moment sooner, whether Christopher would still be alive.

Each time I've met his father, I've seen more of who the son was, in stories, photographs, cell-phone videos: a handsome, vital,

vibrant young man, noted for his kindness as well as his athleti-
cism and intelligence. Brown-haired, brown-eyed, he had a wide,
engaging smile, joyous, full of appetite for life. At sixteen he had
wanted to go skydiving and his parents forbade it; four years later, a
few months before he died, he went. After his death, someone gave
Richard the video, which he showed me earlier this month. It shows
Chris in a yellow jumpsuit, preparing to get into the plane, in the
plane, freefalling in a blue sky with the instructor, and then falling
more gently after the parachute opens, to the green California earth.
The great grin never leaves his face. He was so alive. Then dead.

Martinez had one child; now he has none. He wears rubber
bracelets, the kind given out for charitable causes and campaigns,
stacked atop each other on his right wrist. Each of them commem-
orates a child killed somewhere in the United States by guns, at
Sandy Hook and other mass shootings, and he can sort through
them and speak of where and when each victim was killed. It's an
arm like a cemetery. The parents of these casualties share the bracelets as part of their campaigns; they are a community of the devas-
tated. I have the sense, every time I've spoken with Martinez, starting with a few days after the murder, that he had to do something
to make meaning out of the unbearable pain. He couldn't escape
it, but he could do something with it, and so he quit his longtime
position as a public defender and went on the road.

You can look at the causes of the murder rampage in various
ways. Feminists (myself included) focused last year on the misogyny, the killer's furious sense that women owed him something, that
he had a right to whatever pleasure and adulation they could deliver. Discussion of this crime spree joined the wider conversation
about violence against women. Because men kept popping up to say
"Not all men," sometimes in the form of the hashtag #notallmen,
as in "not all men are rapists and murderers and we shouldn't talk

about the patterns of male violence," a young woman who tweets under the name Gilded Spine coined the hashtag #yesallwomen.

It was meant to say that yes, we know not all men commit these crimes, but the point is that all women are impacted by them. The hashtag went viral in the months after Isla Vista, though Gilded Spine received so many menacing tweets she went silent for a long time. Even speaking up about violence was dangerous, and the men who posted jeering remarks, pornographic images, and threats didn't seem to realize they were all demonstrating why feminism is necessary. #Yesallwomen was perhaps the most widespread of the feminist hashtags that've been, in recent years, the umbrellas for collective conversation and bearing witness about violence and survival.

There's entitlement or authoritarianism in all violence. We say a murderer *took* another's life. *To take* is to take possession of. It's to steal, to assume the privilege of an owner, to dispose of someone else's life itself as though it were yours to do so. It never is. And then there's the gargantuan American arsenal and the havoc wreaked with it. Ninety-one Americans are killed by guns every day in this country; there are twelve thousand gun homicides a year in the United States, more than twenty times the level of other industrialized nations, according to Martinez's organization, Everytown for Gun Safety. It looks as though the gun homicide rate hasn't risen, but that's not because fewer people are shot than a decade ago. More are shot, but emergency rooms and trauma centers are better at saving lives now. The number of nonfatal gunshot wounds doubled between 2002 and 2011.

We are a war zone in two ways. The first is the literal war that produces those twelve thousand corpses a year, including suicides, domestic violence homicides (3,110 women killed by male partners or former partners between 2008 and 2012), other murders, accidental deaths. The second is a war of meaning. On one side are the people who constantly tell us that guns will make us safer, and that we need more guns in more hands in more places, stores, on the streets, in the schools and on the campuses. They constantly hawk scenarios in which "a good guy with a gun stops a bad guy with a gun."

It is surpassingly rare that a person with a gun enters a chaotic situation and, like the gunman-hero in a Western, shoots accurately and effectively, taking out bad people and not harming good ones. The other scenarios involving guns—homicides, suicides, and horrible accidents—happen incessantly. When small children find guns and shoot friends, siblings, parents, we are told it was a terrible accident rather than that's something likely to happen with easily available weapons. The argument in favor of more guns is not about facts but about guns as icons of identity, of fantasy about being dominant, masterful, in control, the same old impossible macho dream of being, as the killer in Isla Vista put it, an alpha male. For hardcore gun advocates, the weapons are totemic objects of identity, rather than the tools that actually take those twelve thousand lives a year.

One response to the Isla Vista rampage is a California law, AB 1014, that allows family members and law enforcement to petition a court to remove guns from the possession of someone who may be a risk to others. The Gun Violence Restraining Order, as it's called, could have prevented at least part of the homicidal rampage carried out in Isla Vista and maybe undermined the whole scenario. The murderer's mother had called the Santa Barbara sheriff's office to report her concern about him earlier that month. It may prevent other murders when it goes into effect on January 1, 2016. Good legislation has been passed in Oregon and Washington state as well, Martinez told me, and Texas and Florida measures to expand gun rights were defeated this year. But knives as well as guns, even a car, were used to harm others that terrible evening a year ago.

There is no easy solution to the violence in this country, and no single cause. As Misrach noted when he contemplated those *Playboy* magazines used for target practice, "Every aspect of our society . . . was riddled with violence." Many aspects are also full of the alternatives to violence: the willingness to negotiate, the love of life, generosity, empathy; these are also powerful forces in the culture. As the murder spree unfolded, people rushed to comfort, shelter, and provide emergency aid—tourniquets, pressure to gun-shot wounds, CPR—to the injured and dying, and twenty thousand came to the memorial at the UCSB stadium that week. But the people who embody the best of us, like all of us, live in a climate in which violence can erupt anywhere at any time.

There is a scholarship in Christopher Michaels-Martinez's name, for English majors committed to social justice. There are memorial events, exhibits, and a garden being prepared for the one-year anniversary at University of California–Santa Barbara. There are laws passed and pending, a vibrant feminist conversation about violence and misogyny. But the dead are still dead, the bereaved are still grieving, and the setup is still ripe for more murders.

The Short Happy Recent History of the Rape Joke

(2015)

Are rape jokes funny? The feminist position a few years ago seemed to be a firm no, and then everything changed. In fact, the rapid evolution of the rape joke over the past three years is a small-scale echo of the huge changes that have taken place in the public conversation about sexual violence, gender, feminism, whose voice matters, and who gets to tell the story.

The gauntlet was thrown down in 2012, when comedian Daniel Tosh was going on about how rape jokes are always funny, and an audience member shouted, "Rape jokes are never funny." Tosh reportedly responded by saying, "Wouldn't it be funny if that girl got raped by like five guys right now?" The woman who had that shouted at her then blogged about it, and her blog and the incident got a lot of attention back then. It was an epoch ago, by what's happened since with feminism and comedy.

That rape jokes aren't funny was an axiom assuming that rape jokes are at the expense of the victim. That they are too funny was insisted upon by some of the tellers and fans of such jokes.

Something horrible happened to you, hahhahha! I'm going to violate and degrade a woman and deny her humanity, hohohoho! It's funny to me and you don't matter!

Sam Morril, who was definitely standing up and who I guess I have to call a comedian, told that kind of joke: "My ex-girlfriend never made me wear a condom. That's huge. She was on the pill." Pause. "Ambien." Because sex with unconscious victims is just so inherently hilarious that America's most celebrated stand-up comic had allegedly been doing it for decades, but we weren't talking about Bill Cosby yet in 2012.

When the conversation started, people drew a distinction between punching down (mocking the less powerful) and punching up (aiming at the privileged, the status quo, maybe even striking blows against the empire). The rape joke as it then existed was all about punching down. Louis C. K., who had lousy rapey jokes in his repertoire back then, remarked that the Tosh incident was part of a larger "fight between comedians and feminists, which are natural enemies. Because stereotypically speaking, feminists can't take a joke." (Or maybe they didn't think feminists were funny because feminists were laughing at them.)

He recovered from his 2012 fumble to do some homework and say, in 2013, that it takes courage for men to ask women out and women to go out with them. Because, "How do women still go out with guys, when you consider that there is no greater threat to women than men? *We're the number one threat to women!* Globally and historically, we're the number one cause of injury and mayhem to women." Which isn't funny, exactly, except for the way that telling startling and transgressive truths is funny. Or at least we laugh when we hear them, out of surprise or discomfort or recognition. Humor and transgression are inseparable, but there are so many kinds of transgression—the kind of joke your eight-year-old loves transgresses against conventional expectations about language or logic and why the chicken crossed the road.

Of course Margaret Atwood had made the same point as Louis C. K. much earlier and more pithily when she remarked, "Men are afraid women are going to laugh at them. Women are afraid that men will kill them." Men with no sense of humor might be the sub-groups who fuel the men's rights movement, Gamergate, and the rest of the misogynistic backlash. I don't believe in revenge, but we are in a moment when one could plausibly mourn that men aren't funny.

Funny women—Amy Poehler, Tina Fey, Cameron Esposito, Margaret Cho, Sarah Silverman—have been achieving more and more prominence in recent years, but it was a man who got to deliver the coup de grace to comedy patriarchy. Hannibal Buress called out Bill Cosby. Finally the time was right to depose "America's dad"—whom a tabloid in 2015 labeled, on its cover, "America's rapist."

Once Buress opened the gate, it was open season on Cosby. At the Golden Globes in January, Fey and Poehler ripped Cosby apart. Alluding to the dark, fairy-tale-based movie *Into the Woods*, Poehler remarked, "and Sleeping Beauty just thought she was getting coffee with Bill Cosby." Fey then did a parody of Cosby's sputtering vocal affectations as she raised the drugging charges another way. "I put the pills in the people. The people did not want the pills." Poehler joined in the mockery, and the cameras panned an audience in which some of the celebrities seemed to think that antirapist jokes were funny and some of them looked like deer in headlights.

And Cosby went down, because serious journalists and survivors' testimony followed in the wake of Buress's opening. Later in January, comedy's august great-uncle, Jay Leno, remarked, "I don't know why it's so hard to believe women. You go to Saudi Arabia, you need two women to testify against a man. Here you need twenty-five." There is a special irony in a major stand-up comic becoming the butt of jokes. It marks the rise of feminist comedy in the mainstream and the weakening of rape culture. There is no clearer changing of the guard than this.

Bill Cosby survived his alleged crime spree as long as he did thanks to a culture in which women had no credibility and little voice, in which their reporting being raped by him just led to further attacks, to his impunity, to the inequality of power. He lost that impunity and much of that power, and the July 26 issue of *New York* magazine, in which thirty-five of the forty-six victims who've come forward to date spoke out and showed us their faces, is basically his tombstone. Their stories bury him. And exhume themselves from the silence of the grave.

Amy Schumer's show on Comedy Central has featured a Cosby skit or two—one in which she's his defense attorney trying to convince the jurors they love "America's dad" and pudding and the rest of it more than they love truth and justice. It calls out people's refusal to abandon something they're fond of or to look at something that makes them uncomfortable. It ends with a twist: an offstage Cosby sends Schumer a drink in thanks and she looks at it in consternation, then tosses it over her shoulder. She knows.

But the great landmark, the epic, the Iliad of all rape jokes at the rapists' expense, has to be *Inside Amy Schumer*'s "Football Town Nights," a parody of *Friday Night Lights* (the TV show about high school football in Texas) and an even more scathing parody of the logic of rape culture. The late April skit features a new coach trying to teach his boys not to rape, to their incomprehension and the resentment of the community. Schumer plays the good wife to the coach, showing up mutely with larger and larger glasses of white wine as things go from bad to worse at his new job.

At the outset the football team in the locker room tries to find loopholes in the coach's "no rape" rule. "Can we rape at away games?" No. "What if it's Halloween and she's dressed like a sexy cat?" No. "What if she thinks it's rape and I don't?" Still no. "What if my mom is the DA and won't prosecute, can I rape?" "If the girl said yes to me the other day, but it was about something else?" "What if the girl says yes and then changes her mind out of nowhere, like a crazy person?"

The high schoolers' arguments are exactly the kind of logic and illogic you get on college campuses and in comments sections, too, the refusal to recognize the limits to men's rights or the existence of women's. This section is followed by an excellent, appalling scene in which middle-aged ladies spit at the coach for not letting "our boys" have their rightful rapes (recalling the real rage directed at any young woman who accuses any sports star of rape and the mainstream focus on the impact on the perpetrator* rather than the victim). The whole skit is a funny rape joke about what irrational, any-excuse jerks would-be rapists are, and how much communities support some of those jerks—about, in short, not rape (no rapes take place in the skit) but rape culture. The tables have turned. Feminism hasn't won, and the war for everyone to have their basic human rights respected isn't over, but we're on a winning streak right now. And it's kind of funny, at times, as well as deadly serious.

Postscript: Since I wrote this Schumer has badly missed the point on race in skits and statements. Her vision (and her scripts) are flawed, and at times her defense has been of the emotional needs of straight white young women rather than what a revolution might do for what it means to be a woman, to be many kinds of women. But she has made a masterpiece or two.

---

* The satirical *Onion* ran this headline in 2011: "College Basketball Star Heroically Overcomes Tragic Rape He Committed."

2.
Breaking the Story

Escape from the Five-Million-Year-Old Suburb

(2015)

Sooner or later in conversations about who we are, who we have been, and who we can be, someone will tell a story about Man the Hunter. It's a story not just about Man but about Woman and Child, too. There are countless variants, but all of them go something like this: in primordial times men went out and hunted and brought home meat to feed women and children, who sat around being dependent on them. In most versions, the story is set in nuclear units, such that men provide only for their own family, and women have no community to help with the kids. In every version, women are baggage that breeds.

Though it makes claims about human societies as they existed 200,000 or 5 million years ago, the story itself isn't so old. Whatever its origins, it seems to have reached a peak of popularity only in the middle of last century. Here's a chunk of one of the most popular versions from the 1960s, Desmond Morris's *The Naked Ape*:

> Because of the extremely long periods of dependency of the young and the heavy demands made by them, the females found themselves almost perpetually confined to the home base. . . . The hunting parties, unlike those of the "pure" carnivores, had to become all-male groups. . . . For a virile primate male to go off on a feeding trip and leave his females unprotected from the advances of any other males that might happen to come by was unheard of. . . . The answer was the development of a pair-bond.

This narrative, in other words, attempts to trace the dominant socioeconomic arrangements of the late fifties and early sixties middle class back to the origins of our species. I think of it as the story of the five-million-year-old suburb. Proto-human males go off—all of them, since apparently none are old or sick or sitting around talking about the fantastic eland they got last week. They go out all day, every day, carrying their spears and atlatls to work and punching the primordial time clock. Females hang around the hearth with the kids, waiting for the men to bring home the bacon. Man feeds woman. Woman propagates man's genes. So many of these stories, as women anthropologists later pointed out, are worried about female fidelity and male power. They assuage these worries by explaining *why* females are faithful and males are powerful: fidelity is exchanged for gobbets of meat.

There was even a 1966 conference at the University of Chicago titled "Man the Hunter" that resulted in a book of that title. In a Google search of the online version of the book, the word *woman* first occurs on page 74, in this sentence: "The non-moving members are less able-bodied persons or the aged, women, and children." The word *gatherer* is similarly rare, though the book is supposed to be about hunter-gatherers. All this would be only a historical curiosity were it not that the stories stuck. People from the mainstream to our own era's misogynist fringe peddle them as facts about who we used to be, and, too often, who we are now.

I learned something about this bizarre fantasy of evolutionary biology at the end of the nineties, while writing a book about the history of walking. I came across the work of anatomist C. Owen Lovejoy, who had been writing about the evolution of human walking in academic journals for over a decade. He deployed a more technically complex version of Morris's tale about pair-bonds: "Bipedality figured in this new reproductive scheme because by freeing the hands it made it possible for the male to carry food gathered far from his mate." The walking thing and the hand thing were for the guys. Women stayed home, dependent.

A much-cited essay Lovejoy published in 1981, "The Origin of Man," actually has a section called "The Nuclear Family," in which he posits that Man the Hunter—who is more monogamous than Morris's hunter with "his females"—brought home meat for his faithful ladyfriend and their children, not the whole group. This seems dubious when you're talking about a big dead animal in warm weather or anything hunted in the company of friends. Wouldn't you be more likely to share your kill and maybe have a community feast? In any case, Lovejoy argues that men provided and women waited. Lovejoy theorized about the "lowered mobility rate of females." In summary: "The nuclear family and human sexual behavior may have their ultimate origin long before the dawn of the Pleistocene."

There is ample evidence to contradict the Man the Hunter story. In the 1950s, Elizabeth Marshall Thomas lived with the people of the Kalahari, sometimes known as the San. They are thought to have maintained, until recently, a more ancient way of life than almost anyone else on earth. Morris's claim about the "extremely long periods of dependency of the young" that kept the females "almost perpetually confined to the home base" is patently untrue in the case of the San, as Thomas learned.

The whole group moved regularly, and families could also move independently of the group. The women Thomas met went out and gathered food almost daily. Children who were too large to be carried and too small to keep up were often tended by someone staying at camp while their mothers roamed. Thomas makes clear that hunting and gathering are not completely separate activities and speaks of "slow game—the tortoises, snakes, snails, and baby birds that are often found by people who are gathering."

Not only were men not the sole providers of food, they weren't even the sole providers of meat. Which is not to say that men didn't bring home meat or that they weren't important. It's just that everyone brought home food, even kids. It was all important. Thomas mentions an exceptional hunter, an athlete who could run down an eland. One day he killed three big animals. He stayed with his carcasses while his wife and her mother recruited others to help carry the meat back to camp. He was truly a great hunter, but he relied on highly mobile women and his extended community for help with his bounty. Thomas notes that "meat united people. A meal of life-giving meat was meant for all." San males didn't hunt as the heads of nuclear families following an individualist way of life; they hunted as part of a community.

The Inuit also shared meat, according to Peter Freuchen, a writer and explorer who lived among them for decades early in the twentieth century. He tells a story about how his Inuit wife furiously mocked a woman who was stingy in sharing a seal her husband had killed. Sharing was etiquette as well as survival. Even among the Inuit, some of the most carnivorous people on earth, women sometimes accompanied men on long hunting trips, because the hunters could die of cold in the subzero weather if their clothing was damaged. Women took care of their food, clothing, and shelter.

The familiar "just-so" stories about male independence also misrepresent the family dynamics of settled farmers and artisanal, industrial, and white-collar workers. Most farmers worked at home—an extended home with fields and orchards—and their families often worked alongside them. The wives and kids of craftsmen often participated in the work in various ways. During the Industrial Revolution, working-class women and children toiled in factories and sweatshops, as they do in the factories of Guatemala and China and Bangladesh today.

Everyone contributes. You could call women dependent, but only if you were willing to call men the same thing. Dependency isn't a very helpful measure; interdependency might be better. Useless and dependent isn't what most women have been, and it isn't what most women are now. Stories about Man the Hunter that contain the notion that men are givers and women are takers, that men work and women are idle, are nothing more than justifications of present-day political positions. A perfect specimen of a men's-rights ranter wrote on social media earlier this year that women have not evolved at all

> because women never worked. . . . And now we have ended up with this cancerous cesspool of female degeneration we all suffer from, day in day out. We need to put women into the world all alone and without help and let them die or survive without any sort of help or interference, so they can catch up on evolution and reach the state of being human too.

His fury is based on a fiction, which would be ridiculous if it were not the extreme form of a widely shared belief, one that paints a fairly sad picture of the human species, with both men and women inhabiting fixed and alienated roles.

There is an interesting contradiction built into this picture: it suggests, on the one hand, that women never worked, and, on the other, that bearing and raising children was such overwhelming work that women were housebound—or cavebound, or treebound. It's as if all women literally had their hands full of babies at all times, like Madonnas in paintings, when it is more likely that those who did become mothers spent concentrated time with babies and toddlers for a while but not forever, and that they led unparalyzed lives before, after, and quite possibly during this phase of motherhood.

Stories that promote the idea of the patriarchal nuclear family have little to do with what women have actually done throughout most of history or prehistory. They suggest that the human condition has always resembled what middle-class, married, stay-at-home women were expected to do in the twentieth century. Even Hannah Arendt describes the female condition as something that involved little more than baby production. She was talking about the specifics of classical Athens, where the women of means, the wives and daughters of citizens, were largely confined to the house, which limited their productivity and participation. Athenian men weren't necessarily producing much, either; food came from the countryside and from far-flung colonies, and most of the manual labor was done by slaves and peasants. Which means that Athenian women continued producing children while the men of the city discontinued producing food. Nevertheless, Arendt writes in *The Human Condition*, "That individual maintenance should be the task of the man and species survival the task of the woman was obvious, and both of these natural functions, the labor of man to provide nourishment and the labor of the woman in giving birth, were subject to the same urgency of life."

Arendt apparently couldn't resist the neat symmetry between "the labor of man" and "the labor of the woman." But we should. For most of history, housework was much harder than it is now. It involved shoveling coal or chopping wood, stoking fires, pumping water, emptying chamber pots, washing everything by hand, butchering or tending animals, and making bread, thread, fabric, clothes, and much else besides from scratch. There have often been women of leisure, of course. But they were usually married to men of leisure. And their leisure was made possible not by hunter-mates but by servants, many of whom were also women.

In any case, leisure was not the primordial human condition, nor is it the condition of most women around the world now. There was a brief era in the Western world when industrialization had made running a household easier and many middle-class women weren't part of the wage-earning economy. You could look at some of these women as nonproducing consumers, though to do that you'd have to discount the labor involved in raising children and keeping a house and supporting a working spouse. This period lasted several decades, but it didn't start five million years ago, and it tapered off when declining wages sent many more women into the workforce.

Right now, in the United States, women constitute 47 percent of wage earners; 74 percent of these working women work full time. Throughout much of the industrialized world the numbers are similar or higher. Elsewhere, women are growing food, carrying water and firewood, herding livestock, pounding cassava root, grinding corn by hand.

Patriarchy—meaning both male domination and societies obsessed with patrilineal descent, which requires strict control over female sexuality—has, in many times and places, created many versions of dependent, unproductive women, who are disabled by dress or body modification, restricted to the home, and limited in their access to education, employment, and profession by laws and customs backed by threats of violence. Some misogynists complain that women are immobile burdens, but much misogyny has striven to make women so.

Antiauthoritarian and feminist anthropologists have attempted to upend some of these stories. Elaine Morgan countered the arguments of the Man the Hunter posse with a 1972 book called *The Descent of Woman*; in 1981, Sarah Blaffer Hrdy wrote a more scientifically solid book, *The Woman That Never Evolved*, which also proposed alternative theories. Even Marshall Sahlins, who participated in the Man the Hunter conference and contributed to the book of the same name, published *Stone Age Economics*, a 1972 treatise that argued hunter-gatherers lived lives with an abundance of free time and food.

But there's an underlying assumption in all these stories: that we are doomed to remain who we were a very long time ago. By that logic you could argue that since we used to eat our food raw, we ought not cook it, or that because we once walked on all fours, this two-legged thing isn't meant to be. Not long ago human beings lived on almost entirely vegetarian diets in some warm places and on almost entirely carnivorous diets in the Arctic.

We are a highly adaptable species. We live in cities and nomadic bands and nuclear units; we're polygamous or polyandrous or practice serial monogamy or take vows of celibacy; we marry people of some other gender or the same gender or never marry at all; we raise our biological children or adopt or are devoted aunts and uncles or hate kids; we work at home or in an office or as migrant farmworkers or visiting nurses; we live in societies where gender apartheid is the norm or where everyone mingles or where the idea of gender itself as something binary and oppositional is being rethought.

There are givens in our biology, and there are particularly common patterns in our past. But we are not necessarily who we once were, and who we once were is not necessarily what the "just-so" stories say. The present is not at all like the past recounted in those just-so stories, but neither was the past. We need to stop telling the story about the woman who stayed home, passive and dependent, waiting for her man. She wasn't sitting around waiting. She was busy. She still is.

The Pigeonholes When the Doves Have Flown

It is not actually possible to say anything, I occasionally notice. Words are general categories that lump together things that are dissimilar in ways that matter; *blue* is a thousand colors and *horse* is thoroughbreds and ponies and toys; *love* means everything and nothing; language is a series of generalizations that sketch out incomplete pictures when they convey anything at all. To use language is to enter into the territory of categories, which are as necessary as they are dangerous.

Categories leak. I was going to write that all categories leak, but there are surely things that can be said of prime numbers or stars that are true without exception. All muskrats are mammals, and all US presidents to date have been men, but so many other categories are complex, containing truth but also contradictions and exceptions to that truth. Even the category *men* is open to question right now, if not usually when we contemplate our forty-five presidents to date.

Someone recently told me that all Jews support Israel. When I objected, he asked if I'd been to New York lately, convinced that this was a clincher in favor of his argument. I remarked that I had, and had just completed a book about the city. One of its maps is about Jews, or rather about how the category *Jew* contains all sorts of people who sort of cancel each other out, Zionists and anti-Zionists, gangsters and humanitarians, Harpo Marx and Sandy Koufax and Hannah Arendt and Bernie Madoff and Elena Kagan; the map's subtitle is "from Emma Goldman to Goldman Sachs," just in case anyone missed the contradictions within the category. My interlocutor was possessed of the idea that Jews are a homogenous mass with one mind, like sentient halvah or slime mold.

The word *discrimination* means two contradictory things. Perceptually to discriminate is to distinguish clearly, to perceive in detail; sociopolitically, it's to refuse to distinguish clearly, to fail to see past the categorical to the particulars and individuals. Racism is a discrimination driven by indiscriminateness or at least by the categorical. Of course this is a categorical statement that contains its opposite. Categories are also useful and necessary to antiracism: subprime mortgage sellers targeted people of color who therefore lost a far higher percentage of their net worth in the 2008 crash; schools, recent studies conclude, often punish Black children more harshly. But these are descriptions of a group's conditions, not its essence.

The idea that a group is an airtight category whose members all share a mindset, beliefs, eventually culpability, is essential to discrimination. It leads to collective punishment, to the idea that if this woman betrayed you, that one can be savaged; that if some people without homes commit crimes, all unhoused people can and should be punished or cast out. The Supreme Court once found that "distinctions between citizens solely based because of their ancestry are by their very nature odious to a free people whose institutions are founded upon the doctrine of equality. For that reason, legislative classification or discrimination based on race alone has often been held to be a denial of equal protection." That was in the case of Fred Korematsu, who protested the effort to imprison him and West Coast Japanese Americans like him during the Second World War, but the court upheld it despite those fine words. Since then, discrimination has been increasingly made illegal, but habits of mind are not regulated by laws.

Antiracist narratives can also be indiscriminate. Some people now like to assert that the Nineteenth Amendment didn't give all women the right to vote, because many (but not all) southern Black women—and men—were denied that right through the 1960s. Sometimes that's phrased as Black women didn't get the vote until the 1960s, though women in some northern parts of the country got the vote before the Nineteenth Amendment. Black women were voting in, for example, Chicago in 1913, while Wyoming gave women the vote in 1869 (and in an even greater anomaly, women of property, presumably white women, were allowed to vote in New Jersey until 1807).

Technically the Nineteenth Amendment gave all adult women who were citizens the right or rather said that none should be denied it "on account of sex"; it's more accurate to say that that right was denied in some places—and to note Native Americans who maintained tribal identities didn't get voting rights until the 1924 Indian Citizenship Act. Are these exceptions big enough to undermine the rule; are the leaks in these categories important to acknowledge? How finely should we parse who got the vote in 1920? On what scale do we sift accuracy?

Paleontologists and evolutionary biologists are sometimes divided into lumpers and splitters—into categories according to whether they tend to read the evidence as indicating a single species with wide variations or distinct and separate species. For paleontologists the evidence they have to work with is scant; sometimes it's contradicted or enhanced by later evidence; even careful study can result in unresolvable questions or contested interpretations. But the judgments we render about each other are often made by avoiding the evidence. Categories become containment systems for some of us. Who we are and what we do is routinely packaged in dismissive ways. All Jews support Israel. All Muslims are jihadis. All lesbians hate men. You wrap up the world in a tidy package, and thinking can stop.

Undiscriminating discrimination also leads to ideas of collective punishment: when you perceive the other as a single organism—Muslims, Jews, Blacks, women, gays, homeless people, lazy poor people—you can strike at any part of that organism. It's what Dylann Storm Roof, the murderer in that church in Charleston, South Carolina, meant when he shot nine men and women in 2015 and explained that Black people were raping "our women," without framing the situation as one in which white men—himself in particular at that moment—were murdering Black women and men.

Any individual woman is liable to be treated as a walking referendum on women—are we all emotional, scheming, math-averse?—while men are relatively free of being thus measured. We don't hear a lot of generalizations about whiteness, and Roof or Charles Manson is not considered a disgrace to his race or gender. Being treated as beyond or outside category may be a kind of privilege, a status as an individual rather than a specimen. It's to be allowed to define yourself and given room to do so. And certainly the refusal to see patterns is an important part of the discourse or lack thereof in our society, where every mass shooting is a shocking anomaly, even when mass shootings come every few days now.

To be free of discrimination is to be allowed to be an individual assessed on the merits. But this becomes a form of freedom that can allow important data to fall through the cracks. For example, the thing that until very recently was almost never said about modern mass shootings is that almost all of them have been by men, and most of the men have been white. Instead, such incidents are usually framed either as mysterious and terribly surprising, or about mental illness and other specifics that make each shooting unique, like snowflakes.

Except when they're conducted by people with Islamic origins, in which case the shootings are called *terrorism* and assumed to be political statements in league with political movements—though in the case of US-born Omar Mateen, who killed more than fifty people in a queer nightclub in Orlando this June, that was just an aspirational idea or an excuse in a miserable life whose idealization of violence and inability to connect resemble that of most of the other mass killers we produce here.

We don't even have a word, let alone a conversation, for the most common kind of mass homicide, which could be called *familicide*, the furious man who takes out children and other family members or sometimes coworkers or bystanders, as well as the woman who's the main focus of his ire, and sometimes himself. The lack of a category means the lack of terms to describe a common phenomenon and thus to recognize its parameters and their commonness. If categories cage, this is a phenomenon overdue for containment.

If there were an epidemic of mass shootings by, say, Native Americans or by lesbians, the particulars of the shooters would be noted, nervous jokes would be made, and the consideration that the whole category should be locked up or shut out would likely be raised. "It is an increasingly horrific fact of life and death in the United States that easily available guns offer troubled Americans the power to act out their grievances in public," wrote the *New York Times* editorial board after one such massacre, as though we couldn't narrow down past the citizenship thing who's doing this. I'd like to see that done not as an accusation but as a diagnosis that could lead to some kind of treatment; if you acknowledge that women are far more immune to the desire to massacre and are less violent overall (with some spectacular exceptions, of course), maybe you can address the causes of extreme violence with more precision. Or at least describe who's scary.

In contrast, every crime by a Black person is taken, by some, to indict the whole category of Blackness. The rise of Black Lives Matter was accompanied by embarrassing white people demanding that any Black person explain the unruly uprisings in Ferguson or Baltimore or apologize for them, or for incidents like them, as though any Black person they might encounter were responsible for all Black people. It isn't possible to be racist without holding an unexamined faith in categories.

Not seeing category can also be a form of insight. There's a story told by a Taoist master I first encountered when I was very young and return to still: Duke Mu of Chin sends out a wise man to find a superlative horse. The man returns with what he describes as a dun-colored mare, but the creature turns out to be a black stallion— and superlative as promised. The horse buyer's friend notes that "intent on the inward qualities, he loses sight of the external. . . . He looks at the things he ought to look at, and neglects those that need not be looked at." In not seeing surfaces, the wise man sees depths. One St. Patrick's Day, when my Irish-American mother was at the state of Alzheimer's where what she saw was not being reliably processed by her brain, she asked a Black man if he was Irish too. He was delighted, because he in fact was part Irish, but people seldom think to ask about the European ancestry of a dark-skinned person.

This is not the same thing as pretending that we can be colorblind in a society where our color affects our status, experience, opportunities, and chances of being shot by the police. Really, what I'm arguing for is the possibility of an art of using and not using category, of being deft and supple and imaginative or maybe just fully awake in how we imagine and describe the world and our experiences of it. Not too tight, not too loose, as a Zen master once put it. Categories are necessary to speech, especially to political and social speech, in which we discuss general tendencies. They're fundamental to language; if language is categories—rain, dreams, jails—then speech is about learning how to conduct the orchestra of words into something precise and maybe even beautiful. Or at least to describe your world well and address others fairly.

Part of the art is learning to recognize exceptions. A doctor I know cites a useful aphorism he learned when he was being trained. It went something like this: "When you see hoofprints, you think horse, but sometimes it's a zebra." That is, the familiar symptoms usually mean the familiar disease but are sometimes evidence of something completely different. A category is a set of assumptions; the aphorism reminds you that sometimes your assumptions are wrong; that the particular doesn't always fit into the general. But the fact that it's sometimes a zebra doesn't undermine the pattern that it's usually horses.

Some of the most furious debates of our time come when opposing sides insist that everything in a given category correspond only to their version of the phenomenon. In recent debates about prostitution, one position at its most dogmatic insists that prostitutes—apparently, all prostitutes—are free agents whose lifestyle and labor choices should be respected and left alone. I've been acquainted with a few middle-class white sex workers. They retained control over what they did and with whom, along with the option of quitting when it stopped being what they wanted to do.

Of course that experience of being a sex worker with agency exists. So do sex trafficking and the forcing of children, immigrants, and other categories of the socially and economically vulnerable into prostitution. Prostitution is not a category of the enslaved or the free, but of both. And undoubtedly there are blurry areas in between. How do you even speak of, let alone propose regulation of, a category as full of internal contradictions? Maybe, like so many other things, it is a language problem, and we need different terms to talk about different categories of people engaged in sex for money.

In 2014, when women wanted to talk about sexual violence, they were often confronted with men who wanted to focus on the fact that not all men are rapists. That subset of men even started a hashtag, #notallmen, as though the central subject ought to be them and their comfort and reputation, not this scourge upon the land. It's a language-and-logic problem: far, far from all men are rapists; we assumed everyone understood, but nearly all rapists are men, and so it's useful to be able to say men rape (and men and boys also get raped, but in much lower numbers than women and girls).

According to Kate Harding's excellent history of rape, *Asking for It*, 98 percent of rapists are men. There are exceptions. I had a male student at an Ivy League school demand to know why I insisted on talking about gender when I talked about rape. Another student there noted that my ideas of gender were "so binary." I speak about gender in binaries because people often operate on that basis. Rape is, among other things, a rite affirming these categories of who has rights and who lacks them, and is often an act of hostility against a gender. None of the fraternity rapists seems to be interested in looking beyond gender, though perhaps doing so is going to be crucial to undoing rape culture. That is, making it possible to see a shared category of humanity that overrides unshared categories of genitals and gender roles.

That we imagine the two main genders as opposite or opposing tightens up the categories and the ways they define each other. The idea that gender is a false binary is a useful one, yet gender is also an inescapably useful thing in talking about who does what to whom and has done over the ages. If, for example, we couldn't note that all of our presidents to date have been male, we could not suggest that the situation should be rectified at some point. *Male* and *female*, *men* and *women*, are how people have organized a lot of their social thinking for a very long time. "Male and female he created them," as the Old Testament says, and its very firm ideas about what men and women are still with us, in case you haven't heard a conservative Christian talk about marriage lately.

We must speak, and in speaking we must use categories such as *Black* and *white*, *male* and *female*. We must also understand the limits of these categories, their leakiness, and that *male* and *female* modify *Black* and *white* and vice versa. The categorical exceptions are important, both of those who were born with anomalous anatomy and those who have an anomalous relationship to their anatomy and the identity assigned on that basis. The Intersex Society of North America notes, "If you ask experts at medical centers how often a child is born so noticeably atypical in terms of genitalia that a specialist in sex differentiation is called in, the number comes out to about 1 in 1500 to 1 in 2000 births. But a lot more people than that are born with subtler forms of sex anatomy variations, some of which won't show up until later in life." They estimate that at 1 in 100. Which means that millions of people in this country do not, even biologically, quite correspond to our categories.

The writers of the text on that website advocate for *intersex* not as a category but rather as a term that allows us to acknowledge that categories are porous and some of us are not contained by them:

> "Intersex" is a general term used for a variety of conditions in which a person is born with a reproductive or sexual anatomy that doesn't seem to fit the typical definitions of female or male. For example, a person might be born appearing to be female on the

outside, but having mostly male-typical anatomy on the inside. Or a person may be born with genitals that seem to be in between the usual male and female types—for example, a girl may be born with a noticeably large clitoris, or lacking a vaginal opening, or a boy may be born with a notably small penis, or with a scrotum that is divided so that it has formed more like labia. Or a person may be born with mosaic genetics, so that some of her cells have XX chromosomes and some of them have XY.

In contemporary parlance, sex is biological and gender is socially constructed; the first is in your pants and your genes, the second in your mind. Perhaps this will change if people are less confined by all the activities and outfits that goes with their assigned gender: the young are going further in dismantling this system that queers and feminists have taken on for decades, both in how they identify and who they desire. (In a recent study, 46 percent of eighteen-to-twenty-four-year-olds identified as totally straight, 6 percent as totally queer, and almost half as somewhere in between.) Some refuse to let gender define them.

My hometown, San Francisco, is where the first man gave birth to a child (that we know of). We tend to think that bearing children is women's work, but a trans man in my town who'd kept his uterus had a child before the much more widely publicized case of Thomas Beatie in 2008. A nice thing about the Beatie case is that the man carried and gave birth to three children because his wife was infertile and he was not. Categories are leaky, and some categories are prone to revision. I never thought I'd get to write "his uterus." Sometimes, not always, the leaks in categories are cause for celebration.

80 Books No Woman Should Read

(2015)

A few years ago, *Esquire* put together a list that keeps rising from the dead like a zombie to haunt the Internet. "The 80 Best Books Every Man Should Read" is a reminder that the magazine is for men, and that if many young people now disavow the binaries of gender, they are revolting against much more established people building up gender like an Iron Curtain across humanity.

Of course, women's magazines like *Cosmopolitan* have provided decades of equally troubling instructions on how to be a woman. Maybe it says a lot about the fragility of gender that instructions on being the two main ones have been issued monthly for so long. Should men read different books than women? In this list they shouldn't even read books *by* women, except for one by Flannery O'Connor among seventy-nine books by men.

The author annotates O'Connor's *A Good Man Is Hard to Find and Other Stories* with a quote: "She would of been a good woman . . . if it had been somebody there to shoot her every minute of her life." Shoot her. Which goes nicely with the comment for John

Steinbeck's *The Grapes of Wrath*: "Because it's all about the titty." In other words, books are instructions; you read them to be a man, and that's why men need their own list. And what is a man? The comment on Jack London's *Call of the Wild* tells us, "A book about dogs is equally a book about men." Bitches be crazy men, I guess.

Scanning the list, which is full of all the manliest books ever, lots of war books, only one book by an out gay man, I was reminded that though it's hard to be a woman it's harder in many ways to be a man, that gender that's supposed to be incessantly defended and demonstrated through acts of manliness. I looked at that list and all unbidden the thought arose, *No wonder there are so many mass murders.* Which are the extreme expression of being a man when the job is framed this way, though, happily, many men have more graceful, empathic ways of being in the world.

The list made me think there should be another, with some of the same books, called "80 Books No Woman Should Read," though of course I believe everyone should read anything they want. I just think some books are instructions on why women are dirt or hardly exist at all except as accessories or are inherently evil and empty. Or they're instructions in the version of masculinity that means being unkind and unaware, that set of values that expands out into violence at home, in war, and by economic means. Let me prove that I'm not a misandrist by starting my own list with Ayn Rand's *Atlas Shrugged,* because any book Congressman Paul Ryan loves that much bears some responsibility for the misery he's dying to create.

Speaking of instructions on women as nonpersons, when I first read *On the Road* (which isn't on this list, though *The Dharma Bums* is), I realized that the book assumed you identified with the protagonist, who is convinced he's sensitive and deep even as he leaves the young Latina farmworker he got involved with to whatever trouble he's created for her. It assumes that you do not identify with the woman herself, who is not on the road and not treated very much like anything other than a discardable depository.

I identified with her, as I did with Lolita (and *Lolita*, that masterpiece of Humbert Humbert's failure of empathy, is on the *Esquire* list with a coy description). I forgave Kerouac eventually, just as I forgave Jim Harrison his objectifying lecherousness on the page, because they have redeeming qualities. And there's a wholesome midwesternness about Harrison's lechery, unlike Charles Bukowski's and Henry Miller's.

Of course all three are on the *Esquire* list. As *n + 1* editor Dayna Tortorici said, "I will never forget reading Bukowski's *Post Office* and feeling so horrible, the way that the narrator describes the thickness of ugly women's legs. I think it was the first time I felt like a book that I was trying to identify with rejected me. Though I did absorb it, and of course it made me hate my body or whatever." Writer Emily Gould described Bellow, Roth, Updike, and Mailer as the "midcentury misogynists" a few years back, and it's a handy term for those four guys on the *Esquire* list who'd also go on my list.

Ernest Hemingway is also in my no-read zone, because if you learn a lot from Gertrude Stein you shouldn't be a homophobic, anti-Semitic misogynist, and because shooting large animals should never be equated with masculinity. The gun-penis-death thing is so sad as well as ugly. And because the terse, repressed prose style is, in his hands, mannered and pretentious and sentimental. Manly sentimental is the worst kind of sentimental, because it's deluded about itself in a way that, say, honestly emotional Dickens never was.

Also, the way Hemingway said shit about F. Scott Fitzgerald's penis size was pathetic and kind of transparent, back when Fitzgerald was a far more successful writer. He's still far better too, with sentences as supple as silk whereas Hemingway's prose is Lego blocks, and with a shapeshifter's empathy for Daisy Buchanan and

Nicole Diver as well as his male characters. (*Tender Is the Night* can be read as, among other things, an investigation of the far-reaching consequences of incest and child abuse.)

Norman Mailer and William Burroughs would go high up on my no-list, because there are so many writers we can read who didn't stab or shoot their wives (and because one writer everyone should read, Luc Sante, wrote an astonishingly good piece about Burroughs's appalling gender politics thirty years ago that was a big influence on me). All those novels by men that seem to believe that size is everything, the nine-hundred-page monsters that, had a woman written them, would be called overweight and told to go on a diet. All those prurient books about violent crimes against women, especially the Black Dahlia murder case, which is a horrible reminder of how much violence against women is eroticized by some men, for other men, and how it makes women internalize the hatred. As Jacqueline Rose noted recently in the *London Review of Books*, "Patriarchy thrives by encouraging women to feel contempt for themselves." Also, I understand that there is a writer named Jonathan Franzen, but I have not read him, except for his recurrent attacks on Jennifer Weiner in interviews.

There are good and great books on the *Esquire* list, though even *Moby-Dick*, which I love, reminds me that a book without women is often said to be about humanity, but a book with women in the foreground is a woman's book. And that list would have you learn about women from James M. Cain and Philip Roth, who just aren't the experts you should go to, not when the great oeuvres of Doris Lessing and Louise Erdrich and Elena Ferrante exist. I look over at my hero shelf and see Philip Levine, Rainer Maria Rilke, Virginia Woolf, Shunryu Suzuki, Adrienne Rich, Pablo Neruda, Subcomandante Marcos, Eduardo Galeano, James Baldwin. These books are, if they are instructions at all, instructions in extending our identities out into the world, human and nonhuman, in imagination as a great act of empathy that lifts you out of yourself, not locks you down into your gender.

Postscript: This article first appeared at Lithub.com, where it got a lot of online attention, prompting *Esquire* to respond: "What can we say? We messed up. Our list of "80 Books Every Man Should Read," published several years ago, was rightfully called out for its lack of diversity in both authors and titles. So we invited eight female literary powerhouses, from Michiko Kakutani to Anna Holmes to Roxane Gay, to help us create a new list."

Men Explain *Lolita* to Me

(2015)

It is a fact universally acknowledged that a woman in possession of an opinion must be in want of a correction. Well, actually, no it isn't, but who doesn't love riffing on Jane Austen and her famous opening sentence? The answer is: lots of people, because we're all different and some of us haven't even read *Pride and Prejudice* dozens of times, but the main point is that I've been performing interesting experiments in proffering my opinions and finding that some of the people out there, particularly men, respond on the grounds that my opinion is wrong, while theirs is right because they are convinced that their opinion is a fact, while mine is a delusion. Sometimes they also seem to think that they are in charge, of me as well of facts.

It isn't a fact universally acknowledged that a person who mistakes his opinions for facts may also mistake himself for God. This can happen if he's been insufficiently exposed to the fact that there are also other people who have other experiences, and they too were created equal, with certain inalienable rights, and that consciousness thing that is so interesting and troubling is also going on inside these other people's heads. This is a problem straight white men suffer from especially, because the Western world has held up a mirror to them for so long—and turns compliant women into mirrors reflecting them back twice life size, Virginia Woolf noted. The rest of us get used to the transgendering and cross-racializing of our identities as we invest in protagonists from Ishmael and David Copperfield to Dirty Harry and Holden Caulfield. But straight white men don't so much. I coined a term a while ago, *priveloblivi-ousness*, to try to describe the way that being the advantaged one, the represented one, often means being the one who doesn't need to be aware and, often, isn't. Which is a form of loss in its own way.

So much of feminism has been women speaking up about hitherto unacknowledged experiences, and so much of antifeminism has been men telling them these things don't happen. "You were not just raped," your rapist may say, and then if you persist there may be death threats, because killing people is the easy way to be the only voice in the room. Nonwhite people get much the same rubbish about how there isn't racism and they don't get treated differently and race doesn't affect any of us, because who knows better than white people who are trying to silence people of color? And queer people too, but we all know all of that already, or should if we are paying attention.

This paying attention is the foundational act of empathy, of listening, of seeing, of imagining experiences other than one's own, of getting out of the boundaries of one's own experience. There's a currently popular argument that books help us feel empathy, but if they do so they do it by helping us imagine that we are people we are not. Or to go deeper within ourselves, to be more aware of what it means to be heartbroken, or ill, or six, or ninety-six, or completely lost. Not just versions of our self rendered awesome and eternally justified and always right, living in a world in which other people only exist to help reinforce our magnificence, though those kinds of books and comic books and movies exist in abundance to cater to the male imagination. Which is a reminder that literature and art can also help us fail at empathy if it sequesters us in the Boring Old Fortress of Magnificent Me.

This is why I had a nice time recently picking on a very male literary canon lined up by *Esquire* as "80 Books Every Man Should Read," seventy-nine of them by men. It seemed to encourage this narrowness of experience. In responding, I was arguing not that everyone should read books by ladies—though shifting the balance matters—but that maybe the whole point of reading is to be able to explore and also transcend your gender (and race and class and orientation and nationality and moment in history and age and ability) and experience being others. Saying this upset some men. Many among that curious gender are easy to upset, and when they are upset they don't know it. They just think you're wrong and sometimes also evil.

There has been a lot said this year about college students—meaning female college students, Black students, trans students—and how they're hypersensitive and demanding that others be censored. That's why the *Atlantic*, a strange publication that veers from progressive to regressive and back again like a weighty pendulum, recently did a piece on "The Coddling of the American Mind." It tells us that, "Jerry Seinfeld and Bill Maher have publicly condemned the oversensitivity of college students, saying too many of them can't take a joke," with the invocation of these two old white guys as definitive authorities.

But seriously, you know who can't take a joke? White guys. Not if it implicates them and their universe, and when you see the rage or get the threats, you're seeing people who really expected to get their own way and be told they're wonderful all through the days. And here, just for the record, let me clarify that I'm not saying all of them can't take it. Many white men—among whom I count many friends (and, naturally, family members nearly as pale as I)—have a sense of humor, that talent for seeing the gap between what things are supposed to be and what they are and for seeing beyond the limits of their own position. Some have deep empathy and insight and write as well as the rest of us. Some are champions of human rights.

But there are also those other ones, and they do pop up and demand coddling. A group of Black college students doesn't like something; they ask for something different in a fairly civil way, and they're accused of needing coddling as though it's needing nuclear arms or needing your wallet at gunpoint. A group of white male gamers doesn't like what a woman cultural critic says about misogyny in gaming, and they spend a year or so persecuting her with an unending torrent of rape threats, death threats, bomb threats, doxxing, and eventually a threat of a massacre that cites Marc Lépine, the Montreal misogynist who murdered fourteen women in 1989, as a role model. I'm speaking, of course, about the case of Anita Sarkeesian and Gamergate. You could call those guys coddled. We should. And seriously, did they feel they were owed a world in which everyone thought everything they did and liked and made was awesome—or just remained silent? Maybe, because they had it for a long time.

I sort of kicked the hornets' nest the other day by expressing feminist opinions about books. It all came down to *Lolita*. The popular argument that novels are good because they inculcate empathy assumes that we identify with characters, and no one gets told they're wrong for identifying with Gilgamesh or even Elizabeth Bennett. It's just that when you identify with Lolita, you're clarifying that this is a book about a white man serially raping a child over a period of years. Should you read *Lolita* and strenuously avoid noticing that this is the plot and these are the characters? Should the narrative have no relationship to your own experience?

All I had actually said was that, just as I had identified with a character who's dismissively treated in *On the Road*, so I'd identified with Lolita. I read many Nabokov novels back in the day, but a novel centered around the serial rape of a child held hostage, back when I was near that child's age, was a little reminder of how hostile the world, or rather the men in it, could be. Which is not a pleasure.

The omnipresence of men raping female children as a literary subject, from Thomas Hardy's *Tess of the d'Urbervilles* to Brett Easton Ellis's *Less Than Zero*, along with real-life accounts like that of Jaycee Dugard (kidnapped at age eleven in 1991 and used as a sex slave for eighteen years by a Bay Area man) or Elizabeth Smart (kidnapped in 2002 and used the same way, for nine months), can have the cumulative effect of reminding women that we spend a lot of our lives quietly, strategically trying not to get raped, which takes a huge toll on our lives and affects our sense of self. Sometimes art reminds us of life.

Hardy's novel is, in fact, a tragedy of what happens when a poor young woman's lack of agency, beginning with her lack of the right to say no to the sex forced on her by a rich man, spirals out to destroy her life in a grand manner. It could be regarded as a great feminist novel. There are a lot of male writers, even a long way back, whom I think of as humane and empathic toward female as well as male characters: Wordsworth, Hardy, Tolstoy, Trollope, Dickens come to mind. (That none of them are blemishless human beings we can discuss another time, possibly after hell freezes over.)

There is a common attack on art that thinks it is a defense. It is the argument that art has no impact on our lives; that art is not dangerous, and therefore all art is beyond reproach; that we have no grounds to object to any of it, and any objection is censorship. No one has ever argued against this view more elegantly than the great, now-gone critic Arthur C. Danto, whose 1988 essay on the subject was formative for my own thinking. That was in the era when right-wing senators wanted to censor art or eliminate the National Endowment for the Arts (NEA) altogether. They opposed art the NEA had supported, including included Robert Mapplethorpe's elegantly formalist pictures of men engaged in sadomasochistic play. Their grounds were that it was dangerous, that it might change individual minds and lives and then our culture. Some of the defenders took the unfortunate position that art is not dangerous because, ultimately, it has no impact.

Photographs and essays and novels and the rest can change your life; they are dangerous. Art shapes the world. I know many people who found a book that determined what they would do with their life or saved their life; if there is no one book that saved me, it's because hundreds or thousands did. There are more complex, less urgent reasons to read books, including pleasure, and pleasure matters. Danto describes the worldview of those who assert there is an apartheid system between art and life: "But the concept of art interposes between life and literature a very tough membrane, which insures the incapacity of the artist to inflict moral harm so long as it is recognized that what he is doing is art." His point is that art can inflict moral harm and often does, just as other books do good. Danto references the totalitarian regimes whose officials recognized very clearly that art can change the world and repressed the stuff that might.

You can read Nabokov's relationship to his character in many ways. Vera Nabokov, the author's wife, wrote, "I wish, though, somebody would notice the tender description of the child, her pathetic dependence on monstrous HH, and her heartrending courage all along. . ." And the women who read Nabokov's novel in repressive Iran, says Azar Nafisi in her widely read book *Reading Lolita in Tehran*, identified, too: "Lolita belongs to a category of victims who have no defense and are never given a chance to articulate their own story. As such she becomes a double victim—not only her life but also her life story is taken from her. We told ourselves we were in that class to prevent ourselves from falling victim to this second crime."

When I wrote the essay that provoked such splenetic responses, I was trying to articulate that there is a canonical body of literature in which women's stories are taken away from them, in which all we get are men's stories. And that these are sometimes books that not only don't describe the world from a woman's point of view but inculcate denigration and degradation of women as cool things to do.

Dilbert comic creator Scott Adams wrote recently that we live in a matriarchy because "access to sex is strictly controlled by the woman." Meaning that you don't get to have sex with someone unless they want to have sex with you, which, if we say it without any gender pronouns, sounds completely reasonable. You don't get to share someone's sandwich unless they want to share their sandwich with you, and that's not a form of oppression either. You probably learned that in kindergarten.

But if you assume that sex with a female body is a right that heterosexual men have, then women are just these crazy illegitimate gatekeepers always trying to get in between you and your rights. Which means you have failed to recognize that women are people, and perhaps that comes from the books and movies you have—and haven't—been exposed to, as well as the direct inculcation of the people and systems around you. Art matters, and there's a fair bit of art in which rape is celebrated as a triumph of the will (see Kate Millet's 1970 book *Sexual Politics*, which covers some of the same male writers as the *Esquire* list). It's always ideological, and it makes the world we live in.

Investigative journalists T. Christian Miller and Ken Armstrong published, in December 2015, a long piece about how police caught a serial rapist (and how one of his victims was not only disbelieved for years but was bullied into saying she lied and then prosecuted for lying). The rapist told them, "Deviant fantasies had gripped him since he was a kid, way back to when he had seen Jabba the Hutt enslave and chain Princess Leia." Culture shapes us.

But "to read *Lolita* and 'identify' with one of the characters is to entirely misunderstand Nabokov," said one of my volunteer instructors. I thought that was funny, so I posted it on Facebook, and a nice liberal man came along and explained to me this book was actually an allegory—as though I hadn't thought of that yet. It is, and it's also a novel about a big old guy violating a spindly child over and over and over. Then she weeps. And then another nice liberal man came along and said, "You don't seem to understand the basic truth of art. I wouldn't care if a novel was about a bunch of women running around castrating men. If it was great writing, I'd want to read it. Probably more than once." Of course there is no such body of literature, and if the nice liberal man who made that statement had been assigned book after book full of castration scenes, maybe even celebrations of castration, it might have made an impact on him.

I hasten to add that I don't think I'm injured by these guys at this point in my life, and I don't feel sorry for myself. I just goggle in amazement at the batshit that comes out of them; it's like I'm running a laboratory and they keep offering up magnificent specimens. Apparently over the horizon some of them got so upset that no less a literary voice than this year's Booker Prize winner Marlon James said, "Liberal men. I'm not about to stop your inevitable progress to neoliberal and eventually, neocon, so let's make this one quick. It seems some of you have a problem with Rebecca Solnit's new piece. There is censorship, and there is challenging somebody's access to making money. This is not the same thing."

And though I was grateful to James for calling them out, I wasn't even challenging anyone's access to making money. I just made humorous remarks about some books and some dead writers' characters in a piece that also praised and celebrated many male writers (it actually praised about the same number of men that it excoriated; you could consider the score even). These guys were apparently upset and convinced that the existence of my opinions and voice menaced others' rights. Guys: censorship is when the authorities repress a work of art, not when someone dislikes it.

I had never said that we shouldn't read *Lolita*. I've read it more than once. I joked that there should be a list of books no woman should read, because quite a few lionized books are rather nasty about my gender, but I'd also said, "Of course I believe everyone should read anything they want. I just think some books are instructions on why women are dirt or hardly exist at all except as accessories or are inherently evil and empty." And then I'd had fun throwing out some opinions about books and writers. But I was serious about this. You read enough books in which people like you are disposable, or are dirt, or are silent, absent, or worthless, and it makes an impact on you. Because art makes the world, because it matters, because it makes us. Or breaks us.

Drinking too much can have many risks for women.

For any pregnant woman and baby

miscarriage
stillbirth
prematurity
fetal alcohol spectrum disorders (FASDs)
sudden infant death syndrome (SIDS)

For any woman

injuries/violence
heart disease
cancer
sexually transmitted diseases
fertility problems
unintended pregnancy

Drinking too much for women includes...

PREGNANT

any alcohol use
by women who are **pregnant or might be pregnant**

NON-PREGNANT

8 or more drinks
per week (more than 1 drink on average per day)

binge drinking
(4 or more drinks within 2-3 hours)

any alcohol use
by those under age 21

Doctors, nurses, or other health professionals should screen* every adult patient, including pregnant women, and counsel those who drink too much. Providers can help women avoid drinking too much, including avoiding alcohol during pregnancy, in 5 steps.

1 Assess a woman's drinking.
- Use a validated screener (e.g., AUDIT (US)*).
- Take 6-15 minutes to explain results and provide counseling to women who are drinking too much.
- Advise her not to drink at all if she is pregnant or might be pregnant.
- Come up with a plan together.

"The best advice is to stop drinking alcohol when you start trying to get pregnant."

2 Recommend birth control if a woman is having sex (if appropriate), not planning to get pregnant, and is drinking alcohol.
- Review risk for pregnancy and importance of birth control use.
- Discuss full range of methods available.
- Encourage her to always use condoms to reduce risk of sexually transmitted diseases.

3 Advise a woman to stop drinking if she is trying to get pregnant or not using birth control with sex.
- Discuss the reasons to stop alcohol use before the woman realizes she is pregnant.

4 Refer for additional services if a woman cannot stop drinking on her own.
- Provide information on local programs or go to SAMHSA treatment locator. www.findtreatment.samhsa.gov
- Consider referral to treatment or recommend Alcoholics Anonymous. www.aa.org

5 Follow up yearly or more often, as needed.
- Set a time for return appointment.
- Continue support at follow-up.

*Learn how to do alcohol screening and counseling at www.cdc.gov/ncbddd/fasd/alcohol-screening.html.

SOURCE: Adapted from American College of Obstetricians and Gynecologists. www.acog.org/alcohol.

The Case of the Missing Perpetrator

(2016)

In a detective novel, you begin in a state of ignorance and advance toward knowledge, clue by clue. The little indicators add up at last to a revelation that sets the world to right and sees that justice is done, or at least provides the satisfaction of a world made clear in the end. If detective fiction is the literature of disillusion, then there's a much more common literature of illusion that aspires to deceive and distract rather than clarify.

A perfect recent example is the Center for Disease Control's new and widely mocked guidelines to drinking. They are like a detective novel run backward—if you read them with credulity, you'd become muddled about what a woman is and how violence and pregnancy happen and who is involved in those things. If you read more carefully, you might learn why the passive tense is so often a cover-up and that the missing subject in a circumlocutionary sentence is often the guilty party.

What is a woman? According to the CDC, all women are in danger of becoming pregnant. "Drinking too much can have many risks for women," its chart tells us, and itemizes them for "any woman." "Injuries/violence" top the list and "unintended pregnancy" brings up the rear. "Drinking too much can have risks for women including . . . any alcohol use for women who are pregnant or might be pregnant." Medical professionals should "advise a woman to stop drinking if she is trying to get pregnant or not using birth control with sex." This in a few deft, simple strokes reduces all women to fertile females in their breeding years who have what you might call exposure to fertile men. It denies the existence of many other kinds of women and the equal responsibility of at least one kind of man. Maybe it denies the existence of men, since women seem to get pregnant here as a consequence of consorting with booze, not boys.

Women is a category covering a great variety of us who fall outside the CDC criteria. Quite a lot of us are past the age of knock-up-ability and all the uncertainty that goes along with it. Even if we do laps with handsome sommeliers in the great barrels of pinot noir ripening in the Napa Valley, we will not accidentally become pregnant. Many younger women are not fertile at all for some reason or other, from long-term birth-control implants and tubal ligations to consequences of medical conditions and treatments and genetic lotteries. Not even with fountains of mojitos spouting up from the ground like geysers will they become pregnant, no matter what. Third, a meaningful population of women are lesbians and/or, when they drink, keep company with other women and not with men or not with fertile men who have unprotected sex with women. No river of whiskey will have any impact on whether they get pregnant either. Finally, trans women generally don't get pregnant even in the presence of a Niagara Falls of prosecco, though some trans men have borne children intentionally, but that's another story and a kind of nice one, much nicer than the one we have to investigate here.

Because here's the really wild thing: how do (fertile cis-) women get pregnant? Get on back to sex ed, sixth-grade style: remember that bit about the union of the sperm and the egg? Because what struck a lot of us when we contemplated the new CDC infographic is that it avoids reference to how women get pregnant. Pregnancy results when particular subsets of men and women get together in particular ways. No man, no pregnancy. If that language is too strong for you, then just say that women become pregnant when a bit of male genetic material is introduced by a male organ (no one becomes unintentionally pregnant by the other methods of introducing sperm or fertilized eggs to uteruses). Oh, and I should mention that that male organ is pretty much always attached to a male person.

A woman can be fertile as the Tigris Valley in the time of Abraham and she's not going to get pregnant absent consort with a seed-bearing man. But if you listened to the way it's often framed, you might believe that women get pregnant on their own. Conservatives assert this when they excoriate women for having "fatherless" children or having sex for pleasure. The antiabortion narrative is often about depraved women having sex for the hell of it and devil take the consequences; the fact that they cannot be having this risk-of-pregnancy type sex in the absence of men is the freaky part of it, a freakiness that is covered up by its familiarity.

A few election cycles ago politician Todd Akin claimed that women did not get pregnant from "legitimate rape." He said that women's bodies had ways of "shutting that thing down," as though uteruses had some sort of remote-controlled door on them. Sometimes overlooked in all the attention to the craziness of his idea was that his comment was in the service of denying even rape victims abortion rights. In the current extremes of antiabortion advocacy and enforcement (like the cases of women prosecuted for trying to induce miscarriages), women have no value in relation to the fetuses in their wombs, though about half those fetuses will turn into women who will, in turn, be assessed as having no value in relation to the next potential generation of fetuses. Women may be worthless containers of containers of containers of things of value, namely men. Embryonic men. Or perhaps children have value until they turn out to be women. I don't know. It's a mystery to me how these people think.

Meanwhile, the mechanisms of pregnancy are assiduously avoided in this mystification-of-reproduction story. First, there is what we could call the mystery of the missing man: it absents guys from reproduction and absolves fathers from what is called fatherlessness, as though their absence from the life of a child somehow had nothing to do with them. (And, yeah, there are bad women who shut out nice men from contact with their kids, though from personal experience I know of more cases of dads missing in action and moms on the run from violent creeps.) Seriously, we know why men are absented from these narratives: it absolves them from responsibility for pregnancies, including the unfortunate and accidental variety, and then it absolves them from producing that phenomenon for which so many poor women have been excoriated for so long: fatherless children. The fathers of the fatherless are legion.

You can imagine a parallel universe of non-misogyny, in which men are told that they carry around this dangerous stuff that can blow a woman up into nine months of pregnancy and the production of other human beings, and that they are irresponsible, immoral, and lacking in something or other—what is it that women are lacking?—when they go around putting that stuff in impregnatable people without consent, planning, or care for long-term consequences. There is not much scolding along those lines, outside of warnings about women entrapping men with pregnancy, which is often a way of describing male withdrawal of responsibility but not of sperm.

Recommendations for women around the Zika virus have been

similar to these alcohol guidelines for women: the responsibility for preventing pregnancy in the presence of a disease that causes birth defects has been portrayed as entirely up to women, even in countries like El Salvador, where abortion is illegal in all circumstances, birth control is not readily accessible, and (like pretty much everywhere else) women do not always have a safe and easy time saying no to sex. Seventeen women accused of having abortions (which is sometimes how a miscarriage is interpreted in El Salvador) are in prison for homicide. It's arguable whom their bodies are thought to belong to, but it is clear their bodies are not regarded as belonging to them. Brazil did get around to telling men to use condoms during sex with pregnant women (but not with women at risk of being impregnated).

This mystification of reproduction is full of missing men and missing access to resources. The CDC's highlighting of unintended pregnancy in the United States raises the questions of how maybe better access to reproductive rights and education and health care might do more to reduce unintended pregnancies than the assertion that all reproductive-age women not on birth control should not drink alcohol (a mandate that ignores how many women get pregnant unintentionally while actually on birth control).

I wish all this telling women alcohol is dangerous was a manifestation of a country that loves babies so much it's all over lead contamination from New Orleans to Baltimore to Flint and the lousy nitrate-contaminated water of Iowa and carcinogenic pesticides and the links between sugary junk food and juvenile diabetes and the need for universal access to health care and daycare and good and adequate food. You know it's not. It's just about hating on women. Hating on women requires narratives that make men vanish and make women magicians, producing babies out of thin air and dissolute habits. This is an interesting narrative for the power it accords women, but I would rather have an accurate one. And maybe a broader one talking about all the ecological and economic factors that impact the well-being of children. But then the guilty party becomes us, not them.

Language matters. We've had a big struggle over the language about rape so that people would stop blaming victims. The epithet that put it concisely is: rapists cause rape. Not what women wear or consume, where they go, and the rest, because when you regard women as at fault you enter into another one of our anti-detective novels or another chapter of the mystery of the missing protagonist. Rape is a willful act: the actor is a rapist. And yet you'd think that young women on college campuses in particular were raping themselves, so absent have young men on campuses been from the mystificational narratives. Men are abstracted into a sort of weather, an ambient natural force, an inevitability that cannot be governed or held accountable. Individual men disappear in this narrative, and rape, assault, pregnancy just become weather conditions to which women have to adapt. If those things happen to them, the failure is theirs.

We have a lot of stories like this in this country, stories that, if you believe them, make you stupid. Stories that are not expositions but cover-ups of things like the causes of poverty and the consequences of racism. Stories that unhitch cause from effect and shunt meaning aside. The CDC extends the absence of perpetrators from crimes by telling women, in their simple orange-and-green chart about why women shouldn't drink, that drinking too much carries the risks of "injuries/violence." Now, falling over and breaking something is a risk of being drunk as a skunk, but since injuries here is coupled with violence, and tripping over a chair is not commonly regarded as violence, it's clear that what's meant is: someone might hurt and injure you. In sane worlds and grammatically coherent narratives, violence has a cause, and that cause has agency and consciousness: it has to be another living entity. Alcohol cannot be that entity, since alcohol doesn't have agency and consciousness.

A tree that falls on you is not violent, though a landlord might be responsible if your ill-maintained house collapses on you.

You drink, you get injured, but who injures you must not be mentioned. It's as though there's only women and alcohol in the room. Even when that someone is the person being addressed: the CDC guidelines telling men that they, too, should watch their drinking notes that "Excessive alcohol use is commonly involved in sexual assault." It's as though there's a person named "excessive alcohol use," or, rather, Excessive Alcohol Use, whose shirts or maybe hip flasks would be monogrammed EAU. We have all met EAU. He is often involved in sexual assault. But here's the point: he never acts alone. Because the CDC is twisting itself into baroque knots to avoid saying "you" or "men" or "drunk guys" or "perpetrators." They seem less worried that someone might get hurt in the sense of beat up or raped than that someone's feelings might get hurt. But people get hurt in part because we don't want to talk about who does the hurting.

Excessive Alcohol Use has a brother named Excessive Alcohol Consumption on this list, and he's trouble, too: "Excessive alcohol consumption increases aggression and, as a result, can increase the risk of physically assaulting another person." EAC apparently acts alone, too, in this narrative, which is a sentence in search of a subject. Whose aggression? Who will assault? Maybe the CDC should jump to the chase and issue warnings about men. After all, men are the main source of violence against women (and, for that matter, the main source of violence against men). Imagine the language! "Use of a man may result in pregnancy or injury; men should be used with caution. Assess each man carefully for potential risks. Be careful about using men with alcohol." Maybe they should come with warning labels? But that, too, would exonerate men from responsibility for their acts, and I think a world in which we don't perform that exoneration so often would be a better one. Domestic violence is the leading cause of injury to women ages fifteen to forty-four in the United States.

The "she made me do it" kind of reasoning is a secondary cause; the passive tense and active violence often go together. A policeman on trial in San Francisco for killing an unarmed man who posed no threat said, "It was tragic. But unfortunately I was forced," though nothing forced him except his own misjudgment. Georgia Black, a victim advocate for more than twenty years, remarked to me, "I can't tell you how many sentencings or parole hearings I've attended in which the perpetrator refers to 'the horrible thing that happened.' Even apology letters to the victim or victim's family state 'I am sorry for what has happened to you.'" It's as though the simplicity of *self plus action equals consequence* is a math problem they cannot solve, a sequence they cannot face; language, loose language, vague language, becomes an out. Things happen.

In the wildlife sanctuaries of literature, we study the species of speech, the flight patterns of individual words, the herd behavior of words together, and we learn what language does and why it matters. This is excellent training for going out into the world and looking at all the unhallowed speech of political statements and news headlines and CDC instructions and seeing how it makes the world or, in this case, makes a mess of it. It is the truest, highest purpose of language to make things clear and help us see; when words are used to do the opposite you know you're in trouble and maybe that there's a cover-up.

Detective work and the habits of perception it generates can save us from believing lies and sometimes show us who's being protected when a lie is also an alibi. The CDC is right to warn about the dangers of misusing alcohol, if not in how it did so. For my part, I am trying to warn about the misuses of language. We are all language detectives, and if we pay enough attention we can figure out what statements mean even when those don't mean to tell us, and we can even tell when stories are lying to us. So many of them do.

Giantess

(2016)

The radical is so often imagined as the marginal that sometimes something truly subversive escapes detection just by showing up in a tuxedo rather than a T-shirt or a ski mask. Take *Giant*, the 1956 film directed by George Stevens. It's an epic, a saga, a sweeping family story, a capsule history of Texas's economic transition from cattle to oil, a post-Western Western, and also an incendiary device. At a little over three hours, it has room to stuff in everything from scenes of a marriage to interventions on race, class, and gender.

It stars Elizabeth Taylor and three gay men, Rock Hudson, James Dean, and Sal Mineo, who orbit around each other uneasily in ways that seem only partly about their cinematic roles. I noticed this fact the first time I watched *Giant*, at a thirtieth-anniversary screening at San Francisco's Castro Theatre. Watching films at the great 1,400-seat dream palace from my mid-teens on, I learned from the sighs and groans and snickers of the gay men with me in the dark to notice homoerotic subtexts, to delight in women with verve, and to appreciate camp and bitchiness and cliché. *Giant* had all those things.

While a lot of my peers memorized cult films such as *The Rocky Horror Picture Show*, and the Castro still offers sing-along screenings for people who can chime in on *The Little Mermaid* or *The Sound of Music*, I can now recite along with Taylor some of her best lines from *Giant*. Taylor is that rarest of joys, a woman who breaks rules and triumphs and enjoys herself rather than winding up dead or deserted or defeated, as too many female rebels have in too many patriarchal plots. The year before my first viewing, Hudson had died of AIDS and Taylor had begun standing up for those with the then untreatable and horrifically stigmatized disease. Her outspoken heroics as an advocate and fundraiser made her in real life a little like the unconquered heroine she'd played thirty years before.

Whenever I see a woman like that on screen, I get revved up in a way that men who identify with Hollywood's endless supply of action heroes must be all the time. Just watching Jennifer Lawrence walk down a Texas street like a classic gunslinger to confront an enemy in the 2015 biopic *Joy* gave me a thrill I get maybe once a year or so. Lawrence's Katniss Everdeen was the hard drugs, as were a series of Hong Kong action heroines and La Femme Nikita long before. Beyoncé's recent videos offer some of the same joy, of a woman who slays and doesn't stay down. Distaff invictus, lady with agency.

The second time I saw *Giant* on the Castro's huge screen, for its fortieth anniversary, I brought my own superb source of low-volume commentary, the performance artist Guillermo Gómez-Peña. He was dressed all in black leather and slumped down in his seat with a hangover. He kept murmuring, almost from the outset, "Rebecca, I do not *believe* what I am seeing." Early in the film, the young Maryland debutante Leslie Lynnton, played by a radiant, self-possessed young Taylor, both captivates and annoys West Texas rancher Rock Hudson, the former by being a flirtatious and lovely woman, the latter by speaking her mind. Freudian motif alert: he's come to buy a stallion—a gleaming black horse she rides magnificently in the opening scene—from Lynnton's father. Taylor comes down the morning after they've met to remark to him that she's been reading all night about Texas, and he prepares to be flattered when she remarks, "We really stole Texas! I mean away from Mexico."

It's a demurely outrageous scene, complicated by the handsome Black butler whose nonplussed facial expression gets some camera attention along with Hudson's choke on his toast. The film, made the year after *Brown v. Board of Education* and its little-remembered parallel case, *Hernandez v. Texas*, is going to take on race in Texas, a white-and-brown affair, though it leaves out the politics of being Black in the South. It's not a perfect polemic, and it falls in the large genre of racial justice as seen from the perspective of a white ally, not the affected population, but it's nevertheless extraordinary for a blockbuster filmed while Martin Luther King was finishing graduate school and Rosa Parks was still giving up her seat.

We really stole Texas. It's an amazing thing to say even now, and as an observation Elizabeth Taylor offers at breakfast to a cattle baron besotted with his homeland, it's an astonishment. It's still a good reminder. The year that Guillermo and I watched *Giant* turn forty at the Castro—1996—we were in the midst of an era of immigrant-bashing in California, driven by various myths about economic impact that shifted the burden of a brutal new economy from its lords and masters to its underclasses. That year was also the 150th anniversary of the beginning of the United States's war on Mexico, the war that ended two years later with seizure of Mexico's northern half, the rich expanse from New Mexico to California that, had it remained in Mexican hands, would have led to a wildly different global geopolitics and, perhaps, poor Yankees sneaking across the border for jobs in the superpower to the southwest. (Texas, of course, had been stolen earlier.) Amnesia has been an important component of the ideology of politicians demonizing Latino immigrants and residents, from the Gold Rush to California governor Pete Wilson in the 1990s to the Republican presidential nominee in 2016.

Hudson's character, rancher Jordan Benedict II, survives the truth in the mouth of a beautiful woman, and a scene or two later they're newlyweds speeding home in his private railcar. First seen riding to hounds across the rolling green countryside of the southeast, she is shocked to find she's signed on to life on the scorched grasslands of arid West Texas. But she adjusts to her surroundings. And makes adjustments to them: she starts meddling with how the Latinos on the half-million-acre ranch are treated, having found herself not only in an arid country but an apartheid one. There her husband rules like Abraham in the land of Canaan. Mighty are his herds, vast his lands. Among other things, the film seems to propose that the great division in the United States is not necessarily the famous Civil War configuration of North/South, but East/West, with differences of manners, histories, ecologies, and scale. It's clear that Leslie thinks meeting people who speak Spanish and not English means she's arrived in another country.

The horse Taylor/Leslie rode with confidence in that opening scene has come with her, so that she's identified with the stud, the stallion, the wild force—a nice subversion of the idea that the East or femininity means ethereal inaction. In an early scene, her husband and sister-in-law insist she's too delicate to stay on the spirited steed or out on the roundup under a broiling sun. They dispatch her in the vehicle driven by James Dean's character, layabout handyman Jett Rink, who falls for her, in part because she treats him with gracious respect (in part because she's the most gorgeous thing the world has ever seen).

The brusque sister-in-law, who lives and breathes ranching and bullying, manages to kill herself and the horse by digging in her spurs and fighting the power of a creature used to kinder riders. She breaks his leg, he breaks her neck; she expires on a sofa, he gets put down off camera. But the film gets to her death scene a little later; a resurrection thread starts before it. Taylor gets Dean to stop at the barrio of shacks in which the ranch's Latino workers live and finds a sick mother and baby. When the doctor comes to oversee the death of her sister-in-law, she violates the segregation of the place by making him go do something more useful—save the life of the infant Angel Obregon (who is played by Mineo as a young man later in the film).

It's a freak: a wildly successful mid-1950s Technicolor film about race, class, and gender from a radical perspective, with a charismatic, unsubjugated woman at the center. True, there were films made then that were further to the left. *Salt of the Earth*, also told from the perspective of a strong woman, had been released in 1954, but it was a diligent film about a New Mexico miners' strike, in black and white, that was suppressed; the lavishly colorful *Giant* got nominated for numerous Oscars and won for best director, raked in huge box office, and generally reached a lot of people. Which is what we would like propaganda and advocacy to do; maybe *Giant* suggests that pleasure helps get you there (as do budgets).

It took another decade for me to recognize that *Giant* is also a serious film about a marriage that is strong but not easy, between two people who survive profound disagreements with forbearance and persistence. It's called *Giant* after the scale of things in Texas, and Rock Hudson is a mountain of a man who looms over everything else, but it could have been called *Giantess*. Taylor's Leslie Benedict possesses a moral stature and fearlessness that overshadow all else: she tells off powerful men, reaches out to the people who are supposed to be her invisible underlings, and generally fights the power. She doesn't lose much either, though she accommodates. Her husband mostly reacts and tries to comprehend. Virginia Woolf once remarked that Mary Wollstonecraft's lover Gilbert Imlay had, in involving himself with the great feminist revolutionary, tried to catch a minnow "and hooked a dolphin, and the creature rushed him through the waters until he was dizzy." Hudson's Jordan Benedict is often dizzy when he finds himself married to a warrioress for race, class, and gender justice, but unlike Imlay he never unhooks himself.

Watching Hudson absorb the impact of a relationship—the realization you might not get what you want, or know what to do next, or agree with the person you love—is sobering, and he plays it well, with complex emotions moving across his big smooth slab of a face like clouds and weather moving across the prairie. "You knew I was a proud unpleasant girl when you married me," Leslie tells him the morning after she's broken some more rules by butting into in a political conversation between her husband and his cronies, the power brokers and election-fixers of the Texas plains. There are a lot of movies about how to get into a relationship, a marriage, about falling in love, and some about falling out, but not many about keeping at it through the years. They quarrel, make up, endure, adapt, beget.

Works of art that can accompany you through the decades are mirrors in which you can see yourself, wells in which you can keep dipping. They remind you that it's as much what you bring to the work of art as what it brings to you that matters, and they become registers of how you've changed. If *Giant* is a different film each decade that I watch it, perhaps that's because I am a different person focused on different things in the world around me. Not that I ever gave up on the murmured lessons from the dark.

How long does it take to see something, to know someone? If you put in years, you realize how little you grasped at the start, even when you thought you knew. We move through life mostly not seeing what is around us, not knowing who is around us, not under-

standing the forces at play, not understanding ourselves. Unless we
stay with it, and maybe this is a movie about staying with it. When
I watched *Giant* earlier this year, for the film's sixtieth anniversary,
the marriage plot was familiar, the power of Taylor's Leslie Benedict
remained a joy, and I noticed nuances that had escaped me before.

The worst imaginable thing happens to our protagonists: they
have a son who grows up to become Dennis Hopper. Hopper's character, Jordan Benedict III, is a red-haired, uneasy, shifty, anxious
man who as a child feared horses and as an adult wants to be a doctor and seems to become one remarkably quickly. He also marries
a frumpy Latina nurse, played by Mexican actress Elsa Cárdenas,
without his parents' knowledge. Guillermo told me when we
watched the film twenty years ago that Cárdenas, a medium-size
star in her native Mexico, was far more glamorous than she was
allowed to be in this film, and that like all the Latino characters
in the film she seemed to be smeared with what I think he called
"shoe-polish brown" makeup to make brown people browner.

Hopper's character refuses to contemplate taking over the half-
million-acre ranch, and though one of his two sisters loves ranching, she breaks her father's heart a little more by telling him she
wants a small place where she and her cowhand husband can try
new scientific methods. In the scene where Hudson's character realizes that he has begotten children but no dynasty or heirs, Mineo's
Angel Obregon, acknowledged a few scenes earlier as the best man
in the place, lingers in the background of the scene. I noticed this
for the first time and realized the film seemed thus to suggest that if
only Hudson's character could overcome his racism, a true heir was
at hand, the man Taylor had saved from death years before. Instead,
Angel goes unrecognized and unacknowledged and comes home
from the Second World War in a coffin. His promise, like that of so
many others, has been squandered.

The film can also be considered as a saga about the shift from cattle to oil economies, and Jett Rink goes from slinking ranch hand to tycoon when his little inholding starts spurting fossil fuel. But it's at least as much about the shift from widely tolerated segregation and discrimination to a nascent civil rights era, and Cárdenas, as Hopper's bride and Hudson's daughter-in-law, is the impetus for the battles that draw in her father-in-law in for the film's finale. At Rink's new hotel, the hairdressers refuse to do her hair; then, at the diner where she, her son, her husband, and his parents stop on the way back, the chef insults her. An ostentatiously humble Latino trio (the actors look as though they rode with Pancho Villa) is ejected from the establishment. Hudson, decades into the storyline, hours into the movie, finally rises to the occasion and punches out the diner's huge chef, who punches him back more effectually. Hudson loses the fight and wins Taylor's admiration for slugging his way into civil rights activism, a rebel with a cause.

This time around I realized that gently, slowly, the movie has denied the patriarch every form of patriarchal power: his wife does not obey and often does not respect him; his children refuse his plans for them, especially the son who refused to carry on the ranching legacy and who marries a Mexican or Chicana (or a Tejana, a native Texan of Mexican descent; the film is a little muddled about the distinctions). Ranching itself ceases to be the great central, pivotal industry that defines Texas; oil has overtaken it and changed everything. Jordan Benedict II, one of the biggest ranchers in Texas, has been denied all the forms of power that matter most to him, the film tells us, and that's just fine and well, for him as much as anyone, once he gets over it. The shift is not just from cows to crude but from patriarchy to some kind of open, negotiated reshuffling of everything, the contested contemporary era.

Part of the astonishment, I realized as I watched the movie this last time, was that this is a film about a man who found he couldn't control anything at all, and he's not Job and this is not a jeremiad. That would presume that he should control things, and that it's sad when he doesn't. It would propose that kings should not be deposed. This film postulates the opposite: the king has fallen—as he does literally in the diner—and everything is fine. That's what makes it radical.

If only white men in general were as graceful about the changes as Jordan Benedict II is in the end. I've always seen the film as about Taylor's outsized character, but maybe it's an anti-bildungsroman about the coming of middle age and the surrendering of illusions, including the illusion of control. The insubordinate son, Jordan Benedict III, has presented him with a grandson to carry on the family name, Jordan Benedict IV, a brown child whose big brown eyes, I finally noticed, are the closing shot of the film. This, says *Giant,* is the future; get used to it.

Acknowledgments
and Text Credits

That there is a war against women was my life growing up in a house full of male violence, thinking I would be safe if and when I left, which I did very young, only to find that now strangers on the streets menaced me. As I wrote in *Wanderlust* (2000): "It was the most devastating discovery of my life that I had no real right to life, liberty, and pursuit of happiness out of doors, that the world was full of strangers who seemed to hate me and wished to harm me for no reason other than my gender, that sex so readily became violence, and that hardly anyone else considered it a public issue rather than a private problem." I have tried to make it a public issue.

This war is so woven into our culture that it provokes little outrage and even little attention; isolated events make the news, but the overall pattern is too pervasive to be news. I have been trying to call attention to it by describing some of its impacts, enumerating them with sentences like this one about domestic violence: "It's the number-one cause of injury to American women; of the two million injured annually, more than half a million of those injuries require medical attention, while about 145,000 require overnight hospitalizations, according to the Centers for Disease Control," trying to understand what hate, fear, and entitlement lie behind the violence, and illuminating how the violence is only the more dramatic manifestation of a system that devalues, dehumanizes, and erases women. It's been ugly work at times, reading countless trial transcripts, accounts of rape and murder, statistics on broken bodies and broken lives—but, as part of the project of changing the world, worth it.

My gratitude is to the feminist movement as a critical and pivotal part of the larger revolutions to make us all equal under the law and in our everyday lives, to guarantee rights and respect for everyone. I'm old enough to remember the ugly old world before there was recourse for domestic violence, acquaintance and date rape, and workplace sexual harassment (an ordinary part of my working experience in my teens), old enough to have seen the world change because of insight and organizing and intervention. I'm grateful to the individuals and collectives who delivered a new world in which we are more free and more equal, grateful to have had in recent years a small role in the work, which will not end soon. Nor will we go back, no matter how big the backlash.

I'm grateful to the older women I met who were the first unsubjugated, powerful, free women in my life: my father's cousins Mary Solnit Clarke and June Solnit Sale, human rights activists since the 1940s and key members of the great, undercelebrated organization Women Strike for Peace from its outset in 1961; Carrie and Mary Dann, the Western Shoshone matriarchs whose land rights struggle I joined in 1992 for a few years of valiant effort and great adventure in eastern Nevada; a few years later, the feminist writer Lucy Lippard; then the great Susan Griffin; and many others. I'm grateful to the young women who are recharging feminism with new vigor and vision, including numerous great writers such as Jia Tolentino, Roxane Gay, Mona Eltahawy, Caroline Criado-Perez, Brittney Cooper, Rebecca Traister, Adrienne Maree Brown,

Emma Sulkowicz, and the women of Black Lives Matter, and many young women I've been blessed to meet because of these writings. I'm grateful to my peers, especially Astra Taylor and Marina Sitrin, fierce feminists, brilliant minds, and dear friends. I'm grateful to the many men who have become feminists, and grateful that we now understand that just as women can serve patriarchy, so can men and anyone rebel against it; grateful especially for the voices of many Black men who understand oppression wherever it shows up: Taj James, Elon James White, Teju Cole, Garnette Cadogan, and Jarvis Masters among them. Grateful to the gay men who have been great friends, allies, and sources of insight since I was thirteen, grateful to grow up in a city that has been a world capital of queer liberation. Grateful to the women in my family raising feminist children.

I'm grateful for the brilliance and dedication of Anthony Arnove, Haymarket's editor, and for the beautiful editorial work of Caroline Luft; for the design genius of Abby Weintraub, who made the title *Men Explain Things to Me* into words so bold and clear that the small book served as a placard and provocation, a design we kept for *Hope in the Dark* and this book, which completes a trilogy that was always about hope as well as violence and struggle; and for the generous good work of Rory Fanning, Jim Plank, Julie Fain, and the rest of the Haymarket team; grateful for the readers who wanted to engage in this conversation about gender and power; grateful for the independent bookstores that have kept my books in reach of readers; grateful that books are still central to our lives, still the deepest way to engage with the thoughts of others in tranquility and solitude.

Special thanks to Christopher Beha, who brought me on as the Easy Chair columnist at *Harper's*, where "The Mother of All Questions," "Escape from the 5,000-Year-Old Suburb," and

"Giantess" were first published; to the *Guardian* editors who published several of these pieces, including "An Insurrectionary Year," "One Year after Seven Deaths," and "The Short Happy Recent History of the Rape Joke"; and to John Freeman and Jonny Diamond at Lithub, where the essays "80 Books No Woman Should Read," "Men Explain *Lolita* to Me," and "The Case of the Missing Perpetrator" first appeared.

Huge thanks to my longtime friend Paz de la Calzada, whose exquisite drawings invoke bodies, beauties, transgressions, and boundaries in subtle ways that enrich and deepen this book. And my friend Mary Beth Marks, one of the kindest and most radiant people I've ever been blessed to meet, a great lover of books, of water, of her many friends and her wife and brother and brother-in-law particularly, died suddenly as we were finishing this book, which opened with a dedication to the young people in my life; let it end in loving memory of her.

Artwork Credits

Artwork by Paz de la Calzada. All images by Paz de la Calzada, courtesy of the artist.

Paz de la Calzada is a multidisciplinary artist based in San Francisco. Her site-specific drawings and installations create intricate labyrinths that provide a pathway from the public sphere into a contemplative realm, thus linking two very isolated worlds. The intricate lines and repetitive patterns of her HairScape drawings cohabitate and collaborate with surrounding architecture, reclaiming aspects of female beauty.

    Paz has created temporary public art projects in the United States, India, Crete, and Spain, engaging with local communities and drawing inspiration from their stories.

    www.pazdelacalzada.com

1. HairScape. Charcoal on Canvas. 46" x 40"

2. HairScape. Charcoal on Canvas. 56" x 54"

3. HairScape. Charcoal on Canvas. 24" x 26"

4. HairScape. Charcoal on Paper. 30" x 22"

5. HairScape. Charcoal on Paper. 30" x 22"

6. HairScape. Charcoal on Canvas. 20" x 18"

About the Author

© ADRIAN MENDOZA

Writer, historian, and activist Rebecca Solnit is the author of eighteen or so books on feminism, Western and indigenous history, popular power, social change and insurrection, wandering and walking, hope and disaster, including the books *Men Explain Things to Me* and *Hope in the Dark*, both also with Haymarket; a trilogy of atlases of American cities; *The Faraway Nearby*; *A Paradise Built in Hell: The Extraordinary Communities That Arise in Disaster*; *A Field Guide to Getting Lost*; *Wanderlust: A History of Walking*; and *River of Shadows: Eadweard Muybridge and the Technological Wild West* (for which she received a Guggenheim, the National Book Critics Circle Award in criticism, and the Lannan Literary Award). A product of the California public education system from kindergarten to graduate school, she is a columnist at *Harper's* and a regular contributor to the *Guardian*.

About Haymarket Books

Haymarket Books is a nonprofit, progressive book distributor and publisher, a project of the Center for Economic Research and Social Change. We believe that activists need to take ideas, history, and politics into the many struggles for social justice today. Learning the lessons of past victories, as well as defeats, can arm a new generation of fighters for a better world. As Karl Marx said, "The philosophers have merely interpreted the world; the point, however, is to change it."

We could not succeed in our publishing efforts without the generous financial support of our readers. Learn more and shop our full catalog online at www.haymarketbooks.org.

Also Available by Rebecca Solnit

Hope in the Dark: Untold Histories, Wild Possibilities

Men Explain Things to Me

Also Available
from Haymarket Books

Capitalism: A Ghost Story
Arundhati Roy

The End of Imagination
Arundhati Roy

Exoneree Diaries: The Fight for Innocence, Independence, and Identity
Alison Flowers

Freedom Is a Constant Struggle: Ferguson, Palestine,
and the Foundations of a Movement
Angela Y. Davis, edited by Frank Barat,
foreword by Dr. Cornel West

Live Working or Die Fighting: How the Working Class Went Global
Paul Mason

On History: Tariq Ali and Oliver Stone in Conversation
Oliver Stone and Tariq Ali

On Palestine
Noam Chomsky and Ilan Pappé, edited by Frank Barat

The Speech: The Story Behind Dr. Martin Luther King Jr.'s Dream
Gary Younge